W9-CGN-589

PREFERENTIAL POLICIES

Previously Published Books

COMPASSION VERSUS GUILT
A CONFLICT OF VISIONS
MARXISM: PHILOSOPHY AND ECONOMICS
CIVIL RIGHTS: RHETORIC OR REALITY?
THE ECONOMICS AND POLITICS OF RACE
ETHNIC AMERICA
MARKETS AND MINORITIES
PINK AND BROWN PEOPLE
KNOWLEDGE AND DECISIONS
RACE AND ECONOMICS
CLASSICAL ECONOMICS RECONSIDERED
SAY'S LAW: AN HISTORICAL ANALYSIS
BLACK EDUCATION: MYTHS AND TRAGEDIES
ECONOMICS: ANALYSIS AND ISSUES

PREFERENTIAL POLICIES

An International Perspective

Thomas Sowell

WILLIAM MORROW AND COMPANY, INC.
NEW YORK

Portions of this book were previously published in *Commentary*.

Recognizing the importance of preserving what has been written, it is the policy of William Morrow and Company, Inc., and its imprints and affiliates to have the books it publishes printed on acid-free paper, and we exert our best efforts to that end.

Library of Congress Cataloging-in-Publication Data

Sowell, Thomas, 1930-
Preferential policies : an international perspective / Thomas Sowell.
p. cm.
ISBN 0-688-08599-7
1. Race discrimination—Government policy—Cross-cultural studies. 2. Affirmative action programs—Government policy—Cross-cultural studies. I. Title.
HT1523.S57 1990 89-49712
331.13'3—dc20 CIP

Printed in the United States of America

First Edition

1 2 3 4 5 6 7 8 9 10

BOOK DESIGN BY PAUL CHEVANNES

PREFACE

The international nature of the issue of preferential policies was unintentionally dramatized for me one evening by a well-educated Maori woman who was part of a group having dinner together in an expensive hotel restaurant in Auckland, New Zealand. The central theme of her explicit argument was the historical uniqueness of the Maoris in New Zealand—and how that uniqueness justified and required preferential policies. But the key concepts she used, her general attitude, the intonations of her voice, her facial expressions and gestures, the body language, the buzzwords, her evasive, accusatory, and retaliatory responses to any serious questions or criticisms, all could have been found in almost any large city in the United States, among the representatives of any of a long list of groups having or seeking preferential treatment. With local variations, similar arguments and attitudes can be encountered from Britain to Malaysia to Fiji, and at many points in between. Whatever the uniqueness of the Maoris in New Zealand, the arguments and connotations were closer to being universal than unique.

Groups receiving preferential treatment are indeed as disparate as can be imagined—from untouchables in India to whites in South Africa. That makes it all the more surprising to discover common patterns in programs for such extraordinarily different peoples, in wholly different circumstances, living in countries separated by vast distances and differentiated by sharply contrasting traditions.

Much of the massive literature on preferential policies, in countries around the world, concerns itself with the morality, sociology, politics, legalities, administration, or goals of these policies. These themes have been amply (or perhaps more than amply) explored, while the *actual results* have received remarkably little attention or systematic analysis. A recurring complaint in the relatively few empirical studies that have been done is the lack of data available. Part I of this book focuses on such facts as are available for various groups in various countries. After some empirical foundation has been established, Part II will explore the beliefs and rationales of preferential policies—and why they so seldom match the actual results.

THOMAS SOWELL

Hoover Institution
Stanford, California

ACKNOWLEDGMENTS

This book, more than most, owes much to the generous support of The Hoover Institution, which has enabled me to make trips to a number of countries overseas to collect research material and have discussions with people knowledgeable about local preferential policies and programs. Initially, that was done in connection with a much larger international study of racial and ethnic groups—a study still in progress—so that it would be difficult to separate out those who are to be thanked in connection with this offshoot of that project. They will be listed and their very valuable efforts and insights acknowledged when the larger study is published. However, among those whose names come to mind specifically in connection with the present study are Professors Suma Chitnis of the Tata Institute in Bombay, Myron Weiner of M.I.T., Donald L. Horowitz of Duke University, Robert Kearney of Syracuse University, Marc Galanter of the University of Wisconsin Law School, Sammy Smooha of the University of Haifa, Robert Klitgaard and Nathan Glazer of Harvard, Dr. Bikram Sarkar of the Commission on the Scheduled Tribes and Scheduled Castes in New Delhi, and Mr. Greg Lindsay of the Centre for Independent Studies in Sydney. Their conclusions on the merits of preferential policies differ among themselves and none can be held responsible for my conclusions. Deep apologies are offered to anyone inadvertently omitted. A special word of thanks must also go to my research assistant, Na Liu, who handled the task of finding and prescreening a vast literature on this subject from many countries.

CONTENTS

PART I

THE RESULTS OF PREFERENTIAL POLICIES

CHAPTER ONE

PATTERNS

What is called "affirmative action" in the United States is part of a much larger phenomenon found in many countries around the world: government-mandated preferential policies toward government-designated groups. The nature of these policies and these groups vary across a wide spectrum. Nevertheless, there are similarities in these policies, as well as differences. Both the similarities and the differences must be considered if the phenomenon is to be understood, much less assessed in terms of its consequences. Maoris in New Zealand, Sephardim in Israel, Bumiputeras in Malaysia, Central Asians in the Soviet Union, and untouchables in India are just some of the many groups designated by official policy as recipients of preferential treatment of various sorts. Indeed, in centuries past, preferential policies toward one group or another have been so pervasive that it is the idea of treating individuals alike which is historically recent and unusual.

In Roman times, no one would have expected a Roman citizen to be treated no differently than a foreigner, or a senator no differently than a plebeian or a slave. Such an idea would have been considered at least as strange during the great Chinese dynasties or in the Ottoman Empire, or among the indigenous peoples of the western hemisphere. But, however recent the ideal of equal treatment of all has been, it has taken hold in the fundamental thinking and fundamental political structure of countries as different as India and the United States, both of whose constitutions have a fourteenth amendment requiring equal treatment. It is the resurgence of official group preferences in the wake of such commitments to equal treatment of individuals which has been striking and controversial. One sign of the potency of the idea of equal treatment of individuals has been that, in various countries around the world, preferential policies have been characterized as "temporary" by their advocates, however long they may later turn out to last in practice.

To keep this complex subject from becoming completely unmanageable, it is necessary to define "preferential policies" here to mean *government*-mandated preferences for *government*-designated groups. The spontaneous preferences of particular individuals and groups for "their own kind"—or, in some cases for exotic outsiders—is an important social phenomenon in itself, but will be noted here only insofar as it is relevant to mandated preferential policies. Some preferential policies are intended to offset these spontaneous social preferences, but some—the Jim Crow system of racial discrimination in the United States and apartheid in South Africa, for example—were intended to reinforce existing racial preferences.

Preferential policies, as defined here, are policies which legally mandate that individuals *not* all be judged by the same criteria or subjected to the same procedures when they originate in groups differentiated by government into preferred and non-preferred groups. This operational definition is used in order to investigate the actual consequences of such procedures, regardless of their rationales or hopes, and regardless of whether they are called by such general names as "affirmative action," "compensatory preferences," "discrimination," "reverse discrimination," or by a variety of more specific terms in particular countries, such as "Africanization," "white supremacy," or "sons of the soil" preferences. No doubt the philosophies, goals, and politics behind these various programs differ greatly. But this is an empirical study of the *results* of preferential policies, whatever they may be called, whether they are instituted legislatively, administratively, or judicially, and whether or not they involve explicit quotas.

The mechanisms and the consequences of preferential policies will be analyzed in an international perspective, with special attention to programs in India, Nigeria, Malaysia, South Africa, Sri Lanka, and the United States. The social context of these programs varies radically among these countries, as do the kinds of groups designated as recipients of preferences. This makes any common patterns among them all the more striking and deserving of closer scrutiny. Among these patterns are the following:

1. Preferential programs, even when explicitly and repeatedly defined as "temporary," have tended not only to persist but also to expand in scope, either embracing more groups or spreading to wider realms for the same groups, or both. Even preferential programs established with legally mandated cut-off dates, as in India and Pakistan, have continued far past those dates by subsequent extensions.
2. Within the groups designated by government as recipients of preferential treatment, the benefits have usually gone disproportionately to those members already more fortunate.
3. Group polarization has tended to increase in the wake of preferential programs, with non-preferred groups reacting adversely, in ways ranging from political backlash to mob violence and civil war.
4. Fraudulent claims of belonging to the designated

beneficiary groups have been widespread and have taken many forms in various countries.

5. Both official and unofficial writings on preferential programs tend to abound in discussions of the rationales, mechanics, and resource inputs of such programs, with a dearth—or even total absence—of data on the actual outcomes.

There are also many important differences among preferential programs in different countries—or even in the same country at different times (the "Jim Crow" era and the "affirmative action" era in the United States, for example). Some of these differences will become apparent in specific discussions of preferential programs in particular countries. What is important is to distinguish these various programs, not only historically but also analytically. Preferences may exist for a majority or for a minority, and the economies in which these governmental policies are imposed may already be largely in the hands of the majority or a minority, or a group of minorities.

Whether for a majority or a minority, some preferences may be "compensatory" preferences, intended to allow some poorer group to close the economic gap between itself and some more fortunate group. Other preferences are intended to maintain the existing economic advantages already enjoyed by a politically dominant group. The latter situation is often called simply "discrimination." Procedurally, however, it follows the same principles as compensatory preferences: Rules, standards, or procedures are different for individuals originating in different government-designated groups. The empirical consequences of such policies are to be analyzed without regard to the labels they bear. If the differences designated by these labels change the consequences, that fact will become apparent. If the differences designated by such labels as "discrimination" versus "compensatory preferences" make little empirical difference, that fact too will become apparent.

This study will focus on preferential policies as between discrete social groups, rather than between men and women. This reflects more than a general presumption that differences between racial, caste, etc., groups are not the same as differences between the sexes. Empirical evidence shows a radically different pattern in economic disparities between the sexes. Empirically, the fundamental difference is between married women (especially those with children) and everybody else—male or female. In Canada, for example, women who never married earned more than 99 percent of the income of men who never married.[1] In the United States, women who remained single and worked continuously into their thirties earned more than 100 percent of the income of single men—even *before* preferential policies for women.[2] Political activists may analogize the situation of women to that of minorities and attribute economic disparities to forces more sinister than domestic lifestyles but their reiterated vehemence is not evidence. Whatever "women's issues" may be and however they may be resolved, they are not the same as the issues involved in preferential policies for discrete social groups. Understanding the latter is a major undertaking in itself.

The analysis that follows begins with those situations in which the same dominant group controls both the economic system and the political system and, in addition, votes itself official preferences. The "Jim Crow" era in the United States and apartheid in South Africa are obvious examples—but an examination of the economic forces at work in such situations can yield conclusions that are far from obvious, and which have serious implications for other kinds of situations.

A more common situation in various countries today is the economic dominance of one group and the political dominance of another. Preferential programs in Malaysia, Sri Lanka, Fiji, Uganda, Nigeria, and in some states in India have grown out of attempts of politically dominant groups to gain through the ballot box what they have been unable to achieve in the marketplace. Finally, there are those situations where a politically dominant group creates preferential programs for historically disadvantaged minorities—blacks in the United States, untouchables in India, Maoris in New Zealand, and aborigines in Australia, for example.

The chapters that follow explore not only the different patterns which emerge from these various situations but also—and more importantly—the economic and political principles which make the results different or similar. Only after understanding these principles is it possible to assess the probable outcome of preferential programs in general, as distinguished from their hopes, goals, or ideals.

CHAPTER TWO

MAJORITY PREFERENCES IN MAJORITY ECONOMIES

Where the same dominant group has complete control of both the economy and the political system, and in addition has strong racial preferences for its own members over others, it is not immediately obvious why there would be a necessity for them to impose laws mandating such preferences. If they wish to discriminate, it would seem that they are in a position simply to go ahead and do so. Yet such laws have been imposed—and tightened over time—in situations which closely approximate this extreme case, in the American South during the era of segregation laws and in South Africa throughout its history. Nor were these racially discriminatory laws mere needless "overkill."

Such laws have made a very real difference and their modifications have occasioned bitter political struggles. How and why they matter so much under these conditions of total dominance by one group is the key question to address. In short, why was it necessary to have laws to *force* racists to practice racism, when the employers, landowners, businessmen, etc., were overwhelmingly from the dominant group and were free to segregate and discriminate on their own? Although this is an historical question, the answer is especially important today, when it is widely assumed that only laws can *prevent* racists from practicing racism.

COSTS OF DISCRIMINATION

The costs imposed on the victims of discrimination have long been a central moral concern. However, from a cause-and-effect perspective, it is also necessary to consider the costs incurred by the employer, landlord, or other economic transactor who chooses to discriminate. When apartments remain vacant longer because minority tenants are turned away, the landlord pays a cost for discriminating. So does the discriminating employer whose jobs remain unfilled longer or can be filled more quickly only by offering higher pay. These kinds of costs of discrimination may have no moral significance (being self-inflicted) but they have serious practical consequences. While economists have been analyzing these costs of discrimination for more than 30 years, outside the economics profession the concept is still so unfamiliar that its consequences may best be illustrated with concrete examples.

Public Transportation

A landmark episode in the American civil rights struggle of the 1950s was the Montgomery, Alabama, bus boycott against racially segregated seating, led by a little known, young minister named Martin Luther King, Jr. But although segregated public transportation was considered part of a Southern "way of life," as if from time immemorial, the historical fact is that it was not uncommon for public transportation to be racially *un*segregated in nineteenth-century Southern cities—including Montgomery, Alabama. Laws imposing separate seating for blacks and whites on streetcars were passed in 1900 in Montgomery, in 1902 in Mobile, in 1903 in Houston, and in 1901 in Jacksonville, for example. In Georgia, a state law requiring racial segregation on railroads and streetcars was passed in 1891.[1] Prior to these laws, individuals either sat where they pleased or were segregated into smoking and non-smoking sections—but not by race.

Segregation into smoking and non-smoking sections is significant because it was done on the initiative of streetcar companies themselves, while some of those same companies publicly opposed the imposition of racially segregated seating by law when such legislation was first proposed. Even after such Jim Crow laws were passed, the streetcar company in Mobile initially refused to comply and in Montgomery it was reported in the early years that blacks simply continued to sit wherever they pleased.[2] In Jacksonville, the streetcar company delayed enforcing the segregated seating law of 1901 until 1905.[3] Georgia's state law of 1891 segregating the races was ignored by the streetcar companies in Augusta until 1898, in Savannah until 1899, and in the latter city was not fully enforced until 1906.[4] In Mobile, the streetcar company publicly refused to enforce the Jim Crow laws of 1902, until its streetcar conductors began to be arrested and fined for non-compliance with the law.[5] In Tennessee, the streetcar company opposed the state legislation imposing Jim Crow seating in 1903, delayed enforcement after the law was passed, and eventually was able to get the state courts to declare it unconstitutional.[6]

There is no compelling reason to believe that those whites who owned streetcar companies were any less racist than those whites who did not. Their opposition to segregated seating was economic rather than ideological. In that era, streetcar companies were privately owned, profit-making enterprises. As such, they resisted anything that involved additional problems—costs—without additional revenue. Far from generating revenue, racially segregated seating jeopardized existing revenue. Organized boycotts of streetcars by blacks—which occurred in a number of Southern cities as Jim Crow laws were imposed—were an obvious threat to profits. But, even in the absence of organized boycotts, the mere fact that many blacks as individuals would find Jim Crow streetcars distasteful could reduce the frequency with which they rode.

It was not a mere happenstance that the economic incentives facing the streetcar companies forced them into behavior consonant with the feelings of their black customers, particularly where their white customers obviously did not feel strongly enough about it to cause racial segregation to occur through market pressures, the way segregation between smokers and non-smokers had occurred. Similar economic incentives have led businesses to resist or evade racial discrimination laws in a number of industries, not only in the United States but even in South Africa. Ultimately, the political powers that be prevailed in both countries. What is important is to understand that *laws* were necessary to get racial prejudice translated effectively into pervasive discrimination, because the forces of the marketplace operated in the opposite direction. Prejudice is free but discrimination has costs.

Looked at another way, the costs of translating subjective prejudice into objective acts of discrimination are different according to whether it is done through political or economic institutions. As with other kinds of transactions, the lower the cost the more is demanded. The amount of discrimination demanded through political institutions therefore consistently exceeds the amount of discrimination demanded through economic institutions. This simple but powerful fact underlies the history of racial discrimination, not only in the United States but also in South Africa, Nazi Germany, and elsewhere. Much effort has been needlessly expended establishing the *existence* of racism—as if it were an easy step from that to discrimination. But discrimination is costly to the discriminator, when it occurs through the marketplace.

Even in the extreme case of Nazi Germany during the 1930s, government-organized boycotts of businesses owned by Jews produced disappointing results for the regime, as even generals in uniform made purchases in Jewish shops.[7] Indeed, the whole history of middleman minorities, such as the Jews in Europe, the overseas Chinese in Southeast Asia, and the Indians in East Africa, is a history of their achieving a level of prosperity which would have been impossible without the economic patronage of majority populations hostile to them. A classic example was the relationship between Jewish and Polish immigrants in Chicago during the early twentieth century:

> . . . the Poles and the Jews in Chicago . . . have a profound feeling of disrespect and contempt for each other, bred by contiguity and by historical friction in the pale; but they trade with each other on Milwaukee Avenue and on Maxwell Street. A study of numerous cases shows that not only do many Jews open their businesses on Milwaukee Avenue and Division Street because they know that the Poles are the predominant population in these neighborhoods, but the Poles come from all over the city to trade on Maxwell Street because they know that there they can find the familiar street-stands owned by Jews.[8]

It is cheap to denounce middleman minorities but costly to pass up bargains in their shops. The economic costs of discrimination to the discriminator take many forms, but what is important is that they are a pervasive and potent reality.

The *differential* costs of discrimination through market

processes versus political processes is evidenced in many ways, in countries around the world. In the American South of the Jim Crow era, segregation and discrimination within the government sector met with no such resistance as it encountered from privately owned streetcar companies. Segregated and highly unequal schooling, all-white police forces, and all-white elected and appointed officials encountered nothing like the resistance put up against Jim Crow streetcars. The difference is that these costs of discrimination in government were not paid by the decision-makers themselves but indirectly by the taxpayers. Discrimination was free for those who made the decisions to discriminate. The pervasiveness of discrimination when it is a free good is in accord with the most basic economic principles.

Employment Discrimination

The market-induced resistance of Southern streetcar companies to politically imposed racial discrimination was by no means unique. The same phenomenon can be found in different forms throughout the history of South Africa. Perhaps the most dramatic examples were the events which culminated in the Rand Rebellion of 1922.

While the whites in South Africa have always been a demographic minority, they have at the same time always been a *political* majority and a majority in the running of the economy. Demographics aside, their position has been exactly parallel to that of American whites in the Jim Crow South, except that the South African whites were even more entrenched in their domain.

South Africa's wealthiest and most important industry during its early history was gold mining. But gold mining was especially vulnerable to the economic pressures of the marketplace because gold is an internationally traded, homogeneous commodity. An ounce of gold is worth the same price on the international market, no matter where it is produced, or by whom. Therefore, any special costs imposed by racial policies in South Africa could not be passed on to the customers in higher prices, but had to be absorbed by the gold-mining companies themselves. There was no escape from the costs of discrimination. The large pay differential between unorganized black mine workers and the unionized white mine workers made the cost of discrimination against blacks very high and provided an ever-present temptation for the mining companies to evade discriminatory policies imposed by politicians who did not have to pay the price.

South African laws and government policies mandating racial discrimination, either in particular industries or in the economy in general, go back before the formation of the independent South African state in the early twentieth century. As far back as 1893, the South African mining companies opposed the first statute imposing a "colour bar" in the Transvaal.[9] The white labor unions favored such policies, which barred non-whites from holding certain desirable jobs in mining. Both white management and white labor unions were acting on the basis of their respective economic self-interests, rather than because of any ideological differences about race or any humanitarian concern for blacks. The mining companies were perfectly willing, for example, to hire and house black workers under miserable conditions or to have the government pass oppressive laws against black workers when these laws enabled the mining companies to get their labor more cheaply. Nevertheless, the mining companies and the labor unions were repeatedly pitted against each other politically as a series of ever stronger color-bar laws and policies emerged over the years.

Industrial disputes and strikes in the mining industry often brought the government in, because of the crucial role of mining in the whole South African economy at that time. More than half the export earnings of the nation came from this one industry, and any work stoppage there was a national crisis. This gave the unions great leverage whenever they threatened to strike unless their demands were met.

Under these conditions, white labor union pressure was able to get stronger color-bar policies in 1903 and again in 1907. Where the mining companies' political opposition failed, they simply evaded the law as much as possible, causing the color bar to erode over time, as black workers were hired in greater numbers and in higher positions than they were authorized to hold under the laws and policies of the South African government and under the terms of the labor-management agreements. To stop this erosion of the color bar, the government began to insist on "a definite ratio" of whites to blacks—job quotas—in the mining industry.[10] These racial quotas were promoted by the Mines and Works Act of 1911 and by a labor-management agreement in 1918.

The falling price of gold in the international market in 1921 led the mining companies into more backsliding on racial job quotas. Despite warnings from the South African government that racial job quotas should be considered "sacrosanct,"[11] the mining companies began pulling out of their agreements and announced that they would hire more black miners to replace white miners. About a third of the white miners lost their jobs as more blacks were hired. The reactions of white miners were immediate, angry, and violent in the mining region called the Rand, leading to what is known in South African history as "the Rand Rebellion."

White miners not only went on strike but also on a massive, violent rampage—burning, looting, murdering blacks, and calling for the overthrow of the government. Before order could be restored, the government had to send in not only troops but also artillery, war planes, and tanks. When it was all over, more than 200 people were dead and hundreds wounded.[12] Four strikers were hanged and one committed suicide. The Rand Rebellion was one of the bloodiest labor disputes ever to occur anywhere in the world. It was also a politically bitter struggle, in which the left wing supported the miners with a slogan adapted from *The Communist Manifesto:* "Workers of the World, Unite and Fight for a White South Africa."[13]

The victory of the mining companies and of the government was short-lived, because the political backlash was enormous. Most of the white miners were Afrikaners, as was a majority of the white population, while the mine owners were predominantly Britons or Jews. Moreover, this all happened within a generation after the British and the Afrikaners had fought a bitter and ugly civil war which left lasting scars. The government that crushed the Rand Rebellion was turned out of office at the next election. The extremist, pro-Afrikaner Nationalist Party came to power for the first time, in a coalition with the Labor Party in 1924.

The new government put in stronger and more sweeping racial discrimination laws and policies, applying well beyond the mining industry. It also implicitly recognized the costs of racial discrimination by providing tariff protection for those South African manufacturers who maintained "the employment of a reasonable proportion of civilized workers"—that is, who adhered to job quotas for whites.[14] The tariffs were to offset the costs of discrimination, which put South African industry at a competitive disadvantage with foreign industries, both in the home market and in the world market. In 1934, the Customs Tariff Commission acknowledged that the "greatest competitive drawback of SA industry is the high cost of white labour."[15] White labor was costly because it was insulated from the competition of black labor.

Yet another recognition of the cost of discrimination was the passage of a minimum wage law by the government that took office in 1924, as part of its stepped-up racial preference policies. Because the wage differential between blacks and whites was the crucial factor making racial discrimination costly to employers, the South African government imposed minimum wage laws for the express purpose of keeping black workers from undercutting the wages of white workers and taking their jobs.[16] In Canada, at about the same time, a minimum wage law was passed for the similar purpose of preventing Japanese immigrants from displacing white workers.[17]

Neither this episode nor the mining industry was unique. Indeed, the color bar was more difficult to monitor and enforce in other industries with smaller, more numerous, and less unionized firms. The effectiveness of preferential policies for whites varied accordingly. Thus, while the new and more sweeping preferential policies brought in by the coalition government of the 1920s reduced black employment only from 44 percent of the workers in manufacturing to 40 percent, their effects were much greater in South African railroads, where black employees were 75 percent of all employees before and 49 percent afterwards.[18] As in other countries, preferential employment policies in South Africa were most effective within the government itself. Over the years, an "increase in the employment of poor whites" in South Africa was "much greater in the public sector than in the private sector."[19] These poor whites were almost all Afrikaners.

Even after full-scale apartheid emerged in mid-century, blacks continued to be employed in the private sector in greater numbers than the official racial quotas allowed. In the Transvaal clothing industry, for example, only whites and "coloreds" were supposed to work, according to the racial quotas which completely excluded blacks. But, as of 1969, 60 percent of the employees in that industry were black.[20] The very sweeping scope and pervasiveness of apartheid militated against its being enforced with complete effectiveness, despite a massive bureaucracy devoted to that task.

South African employers not only resisted and evaded government racial preferences; their business organizations even protested publicly during the 1970 political campaign against government extension of racial quotas.[21] This was not based on ideology or humanitarianism. It was based on the costs of discrimination, which businessmen had to cope with. Official South African government reports on various economic sectors showed widespread evasions of racial quotas by employers, some of whom included government-imposed fines in their normal costs of doing business.[22] During a government crackdown in the 1970s, hundreds of building construction firms alone were fined for violating official limitations on the hiring of blacks—and they were by no means the only ones guilty of this, even in this one industry.[23]

Employment preferences for whites in general and Afrikaners in particular were far more effectively maintained in the government, where decision-makers did not have to pay the costs of discrimination. Afrikaners are 57 percent of the white population of South Africa, but more than 80 percent of all government officials and 85 percent of the army's permanent personnel.[24] This over-representation did not reflect any educational or cultural advantages of Afrikaners over the predominantly British remainder of the white population. On the contrary, Afrikaners were historically among the least educated, least skilled, and poorest of the whites. As late as 1946, the average per capita income of Afrikaners was less than half that of the British in South Africa, though by 1960 this had risen to nearly two-thirds of the per capita income of the British, and by 1976 to just over two-thirds.[25]

In the early decades of the twentieth century, a major preoccupation of public policy in South Africa was the large-scale influx of "poor whites"—overwhelmingly Afrikaners—from the rural areas into the city. These "poor whites" were almost all "individuals who could perform manual work only," who were "largely illiterate and unsuited to skilled positions."[26] Massive welfare state measures were required merely to keep them alive and only widespread preferential employment policies, beginning in the 1920s, enabled them to get many jobs in competition with blacks. As of 1911, for example, South African railroads employed less than 4,000 whites and more than 26,000 blacks.[27] Only after the racial preference policies of the 1920s, together with government subsidies to promote the employment of whites, did the number of white railroad employees exceed the number of blacks.

Government subsidies and government jobs played a major role in the rise of Afrikaners from the status of poverty-stricken "poor whites" to semi-skilled employment and—with the passing years and generations—skilled employment and finally business ownership.[28] Ironically, it was the rise of Afrikaners into the business class in the era of apartheid that caused some of these principal beneficiaries of apartheid to become its critics, now that their new role as employers forced them to confront the costs of discrimination.[29] The rise of influential business interests within the ruling Nationalist Party has been partly responsible for the slow but widespread erosion of apartheid that began in the 1970s.[30]

It was not only formal businesses but also ordinary individuals who evaded apartheid to avoid the costs of discrimination:

> To build a house in Johannesburg meant either waiting for months for a white, expensive, legal building gang, or finding a black gang, perhaps with a white nominally in charge in case an official came inquiring. Most customers opted for the quicker, cheaper service.[31]

Differential costs of employment discrimination arise in many different ways in many different countries. Where medieval guilds or modern labor unions prevailed, the pay scale for a given job tended to be higher than it would be in a competitive labor market and therefore attracted more job applicants than otherwise. Uniform pay and a surplus of job applicants reduce the cost of discrimination to virtually zero, so long as the preferred group can supply all the workers actually demanded. Employer discrimination alone can be sufficient to exclude non-preferred groups under these circumstances, even aside from discriminatory membership policies by the guilds or unions themselves. Given the differential costs of discrimination in competitive labor markets versus controlled labor markets, it is possible to understand the otherwise puzzling anomaly that Jewish artisans were once more prevalent in eastern Poland, where anti-Semitism was greatest, and black artisans in the American South where racism was most blatant. In each case, these were regions where guilds (in Poland) or labor unions (in the U.S.) had less control.[32] In each case, there was *more* prejudice than usual but *less* discrimination, because the costs of discrimination (in these particular occupations) were higher in competitive markets than in the controlled markets in other regions of the country.

Housing

Laws restricting where minority groups can live have a long history. The historic examples which have given their name to this general pattern were the Jewish ghettoes created in sixteenth-century Europe. However, the Chinese in Southeast Asia were often residentially segregated by law as well, as blacks still are today in South Africa. All these represent preferential policies for the majority in the sense of official, government-mandated rules, as distinguished from residential concentrations that arise either spontaneously or as a result of privately maintained restrictions. Whether a particular pattern of residential segregation originates with government or not may seem to be a fine distinction. Historically, however, it is a distinction that has made a difference.

Official policy is both more abruptly changeable when the authorities wish to change and more enduringly rigid when they do not. Jewish ghettoes were first instituted by Papal authority in Rome and Ancona in 1555, in an abrupt change from previous Papal policies, which had hitherto been protective toward Jews.[33] The coming to power of a new Pope with anti-Semitic views was the occasion of the change.[34] Ghettoization policies spread rapidly, though not universally, to other European communities. Many of these ghettoes were surrounded by high walls with few gates. Jews, who might work among Christians in the marketplace during the day, were required to be within those walls at night. Moreover, as the Jewish population grew, the ghetto limits tended to remain rigid and the ghettoes simply became more crowded. By the year 1600, ghettoes in Rome, Frankfurt, and Venice suffered far worse overcrowding than even the worst neighborhoods inhabited by Christians.[35]

Both the abruptness of the policy change that created Jewish ghettoes and the rigidity with which ghetto limits were maintained in the face of population pressures reflect the same underlying economic reality—that discrimination had virtually zero cost to the authorities. Where Jews were allowed to escape the ghettoes, or at least to create new ghettoes to accommodate a growing population, it was often because the costs of discrimination were substantial to the authorities in these particular instances. It was precisely when the financial stresses created by wars or by their own personal extravagances forced European rulers to borrow money from, or with the help of, Jewish financiers that anti-Semitism had a high cost.

The Thirty Years War (1618–1648) was thus a turning point in the history of European Jewry, as various autocratic rulers created exemptions, concessions, and sometimes even privileges for Jews, in order to get the financial backing necessary to wage warfare in defense of their own regimes or in hopes of territorial aggrandizement.[36] It was during the Thirty Years War, for example, that a synagogue was permitted to be erected in Vienna for the first time in more than two centuries and in Denmark for the first time ever.[37] New Jewish communities were permitted to be established and new occupations and markets opened up to the Jews.[38] When the city of Prague was pillaged by the victorious soldiers of the Emperor Ferdinand II in 1620, the Jewish quarter was spared—on his orders.[39]

Self-governing communities, however, continued rigidly anti-Semitic policies—the cost of discrimination to more or less democratically elected local officials being still virtually zero and the cost of concessions to Jews being rejection by their Christian constituency. During this era, "virtually everywhere, the hostility of the towns to the Jews remained implacable."[40] Given the *differential* costs of discrimination between autocratic rulers fighting for the survival of their regimes and local officials with no such military responsibilities or personal stakes, it is hardly surprising that local officials were more anti-Semitic in their policies.

In housing as elsewhere, the discrimination demanded via the political system has consistently outstripped discrimination demanded via the economic system—and not just for Jews. In colonial Kenya, it was only the government's policies which were able to maintain "the white highlands" free of Africans or Asians. One of the key features of South African racial policies has been the attempt to keep the cities as all-white enclaves, with blacks living only temporarily or sporadically in those cities as servants to whites. Yet, even under apartheid, the market has eroded racial segregation in housing, with the result that hundreds of thousands of blacks live in forbidden white neighborhoods.[41]

Not all group segregation in housing is caused by government. Where individuals prefer to live with other members of their own group, residential concentration patterns emerge spontaneously in many countries and many periods of history. This non-governmental in-group preference can also be informally enforced by a refusal to rent or sell to those outside the group. However, these non-governmental preferences exact a cost from the discriminator. One way of offsetting such costs is by creating a cost of social disapproval on those who violate the group desire to keep others out. A more tangible device for the same purpose in the United States has been the restrictive covenant, in which homeowners in a given area legally bind themselves not to sell or rent to individuals from particular groups.

The relative effectiveness of governmental and non-governmental devices for group exclusion may be indicated by the history of black ghettoes in the United States, as compared to Jewish ghettoes in Europe. Except where special circumstances, such as the Thirty Years War, created high costs of discrimination, Jewish ghettoes tended to remain relatively fixed in their boundaries, while the history of black ghettoes in the United States has been one of almost continuous expansion over the past hundred years in American cities across the country. Harlem, the first major urban black ghetto in the United States, was an overwhelmingly white, middle-class community at the beginning of the twentieth century. Moreover, it was sufficiently determined to remain so to create numerous organized efforts to keep out blacks, ranging from restrictive covenants to white landlord and realty group organizations, openly and expressly devoted to keeping blacks from entering the community.[42] Because all these activities were not only legal but also socially acceptable in the white community at the time, they were engaged in openly. One realty company, for example, displayed signs which read:

> The agents promise their tenants that these houses will be rented only to WHITE people.[43]

Despite all these efforts, however, central Harlem changed from predominantly white to predominantly black within a decade, from 1910 to 1920,[44] and this black community has continued to expand. Other urban centers around the country experienced similar large and rapid expansions of areas inhabited by blacks, as massive black migrations out of the South created new demands for housing in the north.[45] With more money to be made from renting the same space to blacks rather than to whites, most landlords and realtors found the cost of discrimination prohibitive. Those relatively few who held out to the bitter end in Harlem suffered financially and some even went bankrupt, as the withdrawal of white tenants from the area left discriminatory landlords with a smaller pool of customers.[46]

The contrast between the rapid expansion of black ghettoes, compared to the original Jewish ghettoes, is by no means the only evidence of the differential cost of housing discrimination through the market rather than through the government. Resort to restrictive covenants, racial zoning ordinances, intimidation, and outright violence to keep out minorities is further testimony to the difficulty of doing so through the marketplace, where the cost of discrimination must be borne by the discriminator.

IMPLICATIONS

Costs of discrimination explain many economic and social phenomena which are otherwise simply puzzling anomalies:

1. The need to impose laws to promote group preferences for the majority, in societies where the majority already controls both the economy and the political structure and already has strong preferences for their own people and an aversion or even animosity toward the minority.
2. The *differential* behavior of sectors of the same society controlled by the same majority, according to whether the individual decision-makers pay or do not pay the costs of discrimination—white resistance to Jim Crow laws in the American South and to apartheid in South Africa being almost entirely a private sector phenomenon in both countries.
3. The far more rapid and continuous expansion of black ghettoes via the marketplace in the United States than of Jewish ghettoes maintained by governments in Europe.
4. The tendency of white South African private sector businesses to employ more blacks, and in higher positions, than the apartheid laws permit, while a recurring complaint in the United States under "affirmative action" policies is that white employers employ too few blacks and in too low positions.
5. The greater pervasiveness and more rapid and sweeping reversibility of preferential policies in non-profit and government-regulated sectors. Examples range from the abrupt Papal policy changes that created the first Jewish ghettoes to the fact that universities and public utilities in the United States were among the leading practitioners of employment discrimination against blacks during the 1930s and became some of the leading practitioners of preferential employment of blacks during the 1960s[47]—each policy having far lower costs to these institutions than it would have had for enterprises competing for profits in the private marketplace.

Economically based resistance to, and evasions of, preferential policies have been common in disparate settings in various countries and various periods of history—whether these were majority preferences in majority economies, majority preferences in minority economies, or minority preferences in majority economies. This widespread historical phenomenon undermines the widespread contemporary assumption that evasions and resistance to preferential policies are *ideologically* based—that is, represent racism or sexism, for example, by employers. Clearly, white South African employers have not resisted preferences and quotas favoring white employees out of antipathy toward whites. When resistance and evasion occur whether the group favored or disfavored is the same as the group to which the employer belongs, there is obviously some other factor at work besides group antipathy. Moreover, political prescription of economic behavior provokes resistance and evasion, far beyond the realm of preferential policies. Smuggling is common in countries with severe restrictions on international trade, as are black markets in foreign currency in countries that prescribe an exchange rate very different from that of the marketplace. Whole "underground economies" grow as government imposes more costs and restrictions on the legal economy. Against this background, it is hardly surprising that government attempts to prescribe an employer's workforce composition, rather than let it be whatever emerges from his own efforts to maximize efficiency, runs into similar opposition and evasion.

The assumption that opposition to preferential policies must be ideologically based is often used to argue for the urgent necessity of such policies, because of such attitudes. But group antipathy is neither necessary nor sufficient to explain resistance to preferential policies. This does not deny that group antipathy exists. The point here is that the pervasiveness and severity of group antipathy must be established by evidence other than the kind of resistance and evasion widely seen in response to all sorts of government attempts to prescribe economic results different from those that emerge from the competitive interplay of the marketplace. Something that happens both in the presence and in the absence of group antipathy can hardly be that kind of evidence.

A related assumption is that preferential policies have had disappointing results in some countries because these policies are enforced (or not enforced) by groups indifferent or hostile to the progress of the intended beneficiaries. This assumption is likewise very difficult to maintain where the majority or dominant group is both the intended beneficiary and the group administering the preferential policies. Preferential policies for the benefit of dominant groups have not been limited to American whites during the Jim Crow era, Gentiles in Europe, or whites in South Africa. Other politically dominant groups who have established preferential policies for themselves include the Malays in Malaysia, Fijians in Fiji, Sinhalese in Sri Lanka, Kenyans in Kenya, and numerous local majorities in various states in India. It is not demonstrable that such preferential policies are more successful than preferential policies for minorities. Indeed, many of the same patterns emerge in majority and minority preference programs.

In attempting to assess the over-all effectiveness of preferential policies, it is necessary to try to disentangle the effects of these policies from other policies and trends at work during the same span of time. Afrikaners in South Africa, for example, clearly rose from the status of an underclass to that of a generally prosperous middle class during about half a century of widespread preferential policies, beginning in the 1920s. However, this was also a period of massive transfers of money, via numerous government programs, from the mining industry and other prosperous industrial and commercial sectors to Afrikaner agriculture,

Afrikaner relief, Afrikaner education, and subsidized jobs that went largely to Afrikaners. Given these massive transfers of resources, the effect of preferential employment policies alone is problematical.

Where preferential policies had no such accompanying massive transfers of resources, as during the Jim Crow era in the American South, there was no such dramatic improvement in the relative economic position of Southern whites compared to other whites in regions without Jim Crow laws. On the contrary, the economic condition of whites in the South tended to lag behind that of other whites in regions without Jim Crow laws. The black-white income differential was greater in the South, but was not widening over time, as it did in South Africa after preferential policies were instituted in the 1920s. It is likewise questionable whether anti-Semitic policies in Europe benefited Gentiles. Many countries and regions of Europe prospered from the economic activities of the Jews and declined after they emigrated or were expelled.

In short, preferential policies are not zero-sum games in which what is lost by one group is gained by another. What the actual result has been must be examined in each situation. Because there are often net gains to be made by easing or eliminating discriminatory policies, autocratic rulers were often protectors of Jews, even in anti-Semitic countries with official policies restricting or barring Jews. Although Catherine the Great banned Jews from immigrating into Russia, in her later efforts to attract much-needed foreign skills from Western Europe, including "some merchant people," she wrote to one of her officials that people in the occupations being sought should be given passports "not mentioning their nationality and without inquiring into their confession." To the formal Russian text of this message she added a postscript in German saying, "If you don't understand me, it will not be my fault" and "keep all this secret." In the wake of this message, Jews began to be recruited as immigrants to Russia, even though, as an historian has noted, "throughout the whole transaction any reference to Jewishness was scrupulously avoided."[48] In short, even rulers may seek to evade their own preferential policies, when it is impolitic to repeal them and counterproductive to follow them.

CHAPTER THREE

MAJORITY PREFERENCES IN MINORITY ECONOMIES

In a number of countries, neither the demographic majority nor the political majority is dominant in the economy, which is largely in the hands of one or more ethnic minorities and/or foreign businessmen or investors. Nevertheless, the arguments advanced for preferences in these circumstances are often very similar to those advanced under very different conditions.

The widely known and emotionally powerful history of blacks in the United States has led many other groups to analogize their situation to that of blacks, as a politically effective way of seeking preferential treatment. This approach has been used, not only in the United States, but also in other countries around the world. Where the group seeking preferences is indigenous—as in Burma, Fiji, Malaysia, Sri Lanka, New Zealand, or in India's states of Punjab, Bihar, or Assam—they have analogized themselves to the American Indians.[1] Often, however, these groups' circumstances are not only radically different from those of either American Negroes or American Indians, but also collectively fall into a very distinctive pattern. This pattern has implications that reach well beyond these indigenous groups and offer insight into both the rhetoric and the logic of preferential policies.

The claim of a need and a right to preferential treatment is often made in societies where the economy—or at least the commercial or non-agricultural part of it—is largely in the hands of an ethnic minority, noticeably more prosperous than the majority group that is seeking government-mandated preferences. These economically dominant minorities have, at various periods of history, included the Germans in Latvia, Gujaratis from India in several countries in East Africa, Jews in parts of eastern Europe, and Chinese in a number of countries in Southeast Asia. Sometimes different groups dominate different regions or different industries in a country where the majority population plays little role in the modern, industrial, or commercial economy. At one time that was the situation in Brazil, where German, Japanese, Italian, and other immigrants pioneered and almost wholly controlled many industries. Malays have played little role in the economic development and modernization of their country, either as owners, investors, or even workers in the country's leading industries. In some oil-rich states of the Middle East, half or more of their current labor force is foreign, usually Asians.

Sometimes the economically active foreign elements have been more prosperous than the indigenous population from the beginning. But, very often, an outside group has come into the country precisely because of the poverty of their native land or their own poverty in it (Chinese, southern Italians, Tamils from India, Scots in centuries past, Lebanese, Japanese emigrants in the nineteenth and early twentieth centuries). Sometimes they were fleeing from war or its aftermath (Volga Germans in Czarist Russia, the "boat people" from Vietnam) or from persecution (Jews, Armenians, Huguenots). Often groups from less fertile regions of the same country migrate to other regions and become more prosperous than those indigenous to those regions (Ibos in Nigeria, Toba Batak in Indonesia).[2]

A very common situation in countries around the world

has been one in which the indigenous majority was at one point sufficiently more prosperous and secure to disdain the kind of jobs which the newcomers took. Thais would not pull rickshaws in Siam, but the Chinese did. In colonial Malaya, Malays by and large disdained the hard work and harsh discipline endured by coolie laborers from India and China in the foreign-owned tin mines and on the foreign-owned rubber plantations. Similarly, laborers had to be transported thousands of miles from India to do plantation work in Fiji, East Africa, or British Guiana because the local majorities in these places refused to subject themselves to the working conditions imposed by foreign employers. Even in small-scale agriculture, newcomers have in various places taken over land left idle by the local majority as unproductive "wasteland" and prospered farming it. Many Italians got a foothold in truck-farming this way, both in the United States and in Australia.[3] The Sikhs did the same in India's state of Bihar, to the envy and resentment of the Biharians. In nineteenth-century Latin America, foreigners were deliberately sought by governments to perform the arduous task of opening up virgin lands to agriculture, after the local population refused to do it. This role was played by Japanese farmers in Paraguay's Chaco region and by Germans and Italians, as well as Japanese, in southern Brazil.

In short, majorities who were at one point in history well off enough to pass up opportunities which others seized, often in desperation, have in later years depicted themselves as "disadvantaged" because the incoming minorities have eventually risen above them on the economic scale. This raises a more general question as to the actual meaning of "disadvantaged"—whether it refers to fewer opportunities or to a failure to use those opportunities as effectively as other groups.

Thrift, for example, has long been a characteristic of some groups leading a precarious existence (Scots, Chinese, Jews) and far less so among groups well supplied by nature with an assured subsistence (Malays, Fijians, Assamese). Thrifty groups entering essentially non-thrifty societies, even at the bottom, often rise economically above the local majorities. The inherent ambiguity of the concept of "disadvantaged" becomes more pronounced in this situation, where the minority is disadvantaged in terms of initial *opportunity,* while the indigenous majority is disadvantaged if that term means simply statistical *end-results.*

Sometimes the advantages and disadvantages conferred by nature are compounded by the advantages and disadvantages conferred by man, as when the British colonial officials in Malaya offered educational facilities to the Malays while the Chinese had to provide their own[4]—but the *results* were that the Chinese minority had an absolute majority of the university students in independent Malaysia as late as the 1960s.[5] More than semantic issues are involved in the Malays' depiction of themselves as "disadvantaged." Their situation is wholly different from that of American Negroes, who were once denied admission to many schools and received far lower per-pupil expenditures where they did go to school. The rhetoric of "disadvantage" is invoked politically to cover radically different situations.

The automatic equating of statistical disparities with "disadvantage" can also outlive historical reality for those groups that have in fact been historically disadvantaged in every sense. Because patterns of behavior differ so greatly among social groups, advantaged and disadvantaged cannot be reduced to mere statistical meanings. Some groups in various parts of the world have indeed been seriously disadvantaged relative to others, but there is no way to determine that, if the word "disadvantaged" becomes simply a synonym for substandard end-results. For practical policy-making, there is also no way to know when the removal of disadvantages must be supplemented by other—and very different—actions designed to improve performance, if all substandard performances are covered by the blanket word "disadvantage."

The point here is not to say whether disadvantages or substandard performances are usually the reason for groups' having substandard results. The point is to sharply distinguish the two concepts so that the issue can be faced empirically in specific cases, rather than being defined away by automatically equating statistical disparities with disadvantages. In many parts of the world, the less successful groups themselves recognize that their own deficiencies are an integral part of their problems. Often majority group leaders proclaim their group's inability to compete on even terms with the minority, as a justification for preferential policies. For example, in Nigeria, the fear was expressed that "the less well educated people of the North will be swamped by the thrusting people of the South." In Malaysia it was similarly said: "Malaysia has far too many non-Malay citizens who can swamp the Malays the moment protection is removed."[6] Often ethnic leaders tell their own people that their performance does not measure up, that they should emulate the more successful minorities in their midst—as a Sinhalese leader exhorted in Sri Lanka, as Maharashtrians were exhorted to do in Bombay, Fijians in Fiji, Creoles in Guyana, the Lulua in Zaire, the Assamese in Assam, and others.[7] In this context, preferential policies are often urged as a temporary expedient,[8] to enable those behind to "catch up." What the actual consequences of such policies are is another question to be investigated empirically.

MALAYSIA

Official preferential policies in Malaysia go back well before the country's independence in 1957. Even when it was the British colony of Malaya, there were severe restrictions on non-Malays owning land and, as noted above, the colonial government provided education for Malays while leaving the large Chinese minority to provide their own. The Chinese, though initially largely illiterate as well as destitute, nevertheless proceeded to build their own educational system as they advanced economically.

One of the most remarkable books ever written by an advocate of preferential policies was *The Malay Dilemma* by Dr. Mahatir bin Mohamad, a Malay leader later destined to become Prime Minister. He detailed the natural advantages of the Malays and candidly admitted that they simply could not compete with the Chinese. According to Dr. Mahatir, the Malay culture evolved in a world where there was "plenty of land for everyone," where the "lush tropical plains" provided "plentiful sources of food" and where there was "a lot of free time" left throughout the year after the modest requirements of rice cultivation.[9] By contrast, countries like China—often facing hunger and starvation—produced "hardened and resourceful" people. When the Chinese immigrants competed with the indigenous Malays it was the Malays who invariably lost out: "Whatever the Malays could do, the Chinese could do better and more cheaply," according to Dr. Mahatir.[10]

The hard facts bear out this conclusion in industry after industry, as well as in education. Over the years, the Chinese came ultimately to own more than four-fifths of all the retail establishments in Malaysia,[11] for example. Of all the corporate equity capital invested in Malaysia in 1970, about three-fifths was foreign-owned, with the Chinese owning about three-fifths of the remaining domestically owned corporate investment.[12] When admission to the University of Malaya was determined solely on the basis of examination results, only 20 percent of the students admitted were Malays, with most of the non-Malays being Chinese.[13] In the more difficult mathematical, scientific, and technological fields, the disparities between the Chinese and the Malays were even greater. During the entire decade of the 1960s, for example, the Chinese received 1,488 Bachelor of Science degrees, compared to 69 for the Malays, and 408 Bachelor's degrees in engineering, compared to 4 for the Malays.[14]

Demographically, the Malays were a little more than half the population and the Chinese a little more than a third. Politically, the Malays have been overwhelmingly dominant because the weighting of votes favors them and the constitution ensures their preferential access to government employment.

The modest number of preferential policies for Malays during the colonial era expanded after independence to include "Malaysianization" of government employment. Even here, however, though the Malays dominated general government employment, including administrative and non-professional occupations, the Chinese and the Indians for some time continued to dominate the scientific, professional, and technical branches of government.[15] A further escalation of preferential policies for Malays occurred after the race riots of May 1969, in which Malays unleashed mob violence against the Chinese. The Malay government promulgated its "New Economic Policy," designed to achieve what it called "racial balance." In the government's own words:

> If racial balance in the employment field is to be achieved such that the proportion of the various races in employment in the major sectors of the economy reflects the racial composition of the labour force, all racial groups benefit fully from full employment and existing differentials in *per capita* income between the various races are narrowed, then inter-sectorial movements of labour,

as well as movements to higher productivity activities within sectors, of a sizeable order will be necessary.[16]

Beneficiaries and Losers

This ambitious new program spread preferences to the private sector, including foreign-owned enterprises, and expanded government preferences to include loans and admissions to higher education. Although the government assured "other Malaysians" that their plans to advance the indigenous Bumiputeras or "sons of the soil" would not adversely affect non-Malays,[17] these non-Malays often suffered not only a relative but also an absolute decline. While the police and the armed forces expanded substantially between 1969–70 and 1974–80, the number of non-Malays in both declined absolutely.[18] Likewise, at the University of Malaya, the number of Chinese students declined absolutely between 1970 and 1980,[19] even though the total number of students there was rising.[20] Indeed for Malaysian higher education as a whole, the total number of Chinese students receiving degrees declined between 1970 and 1980,[21] even though the total number of degree recipients more than doubled.[22]

Who gained and who lost in these and other preferential policies? An empirical study of the actual consequences of these policies concluded that "at most 5 per cent" of the Malays benefited from such policies.[23] While the statistical representation of Malays on corporate boards of directors in Malaysia rose under preferential policies,[24] so did the proportion of Malays among the population living below the official poverty line.[25] Income inequality among Malays increased under preferential policies, with the income share of the top 10 percent rising from 42 percent to 53 percent of all income received by all Malays.[26] Dr. Mahatir bin Mohamad has bluntly admitted such consequences of preferential policies, but has attempted to justify them:

> These few Malays, for they are still only very few, have waxed rich not because of themselves but because of the policy of a government supported by a huge majority of poor Malays. It would seem that the efforts of the poor Malays have gone to enrich a select few of their own people. The poor Malays themselves have not gained one iota. But if these few Malays are not enriched the poor Malays will not gain either. It is the Chinese who will continue to live in huge houses and regard the Malays as only fit to drive their cars. With the existence of the few rich Malays at least the poor can say their fate is not entirely to serve rich non-Malays. From the point of view of racial ego, and this ego is still strong, the unseemly existence of Malay tycoons is essential.[27]

In short, the Malay masses provided the political support for preferential policies that benefited the Malay elite—in the name of the masses. This pattern is by no means confined to Malaysia, as subsequent chapters will show. Quite aside from intragroup consequences of preferential policies is the question of intergroup differences. Over a considerable span of years, a variety of studies using a variety of methods have shown the Chinese to be earning roughly double the income of the Malays.[28] Partly this reflects the greater urbanization of the Chinese and to that extent overstates the real economic differences, insofar as urban dwellers pay for some goods that rural dwellers supply for themselves. However, the official government figures, which do not take this into account, seem to indicate a relative increase in the income of Malays as a percentage of the income of Chinese:

Malay Median Income as Percentage of Chinese Median Income

1970	1973	1976	1979	1984
44%	45%	44%	47%	57%

Source: *Fourth Malaysia Plan*, p. 56; *Fifth Malaysia Plan*, p. 99

While these relative income changes look significant, they are hardly dramatic, even as gross statistics. They mean somewhat less in the light of the increased urbanization of the Malays over these years, rising from 27 percent urban in 1970 to 37 percent urban in 1985.[29] With the Chinese sending both their capital and their young people overseas, it is not at all clear how much of the declining income differentials are due directly to preferential policies, rather than to a changing mix of people in Malaysia. In 1980 nearly 40,000 students from Malaysia were studying overseas, three-fifths of them Chinese.[30] By 1985 there were approximately 60,000 students from Malaysia studying overseas—as many as were enrolled in degree programs in Malaysia itself.[31] More than half of all the Indians from Malaysia seeking degrees did so overseas.[32] In addition, more than 10,000 students from Malaysia were in Singapore merely for secondary school,[33] no doubt to escape compulsory Malay language instruction in schools that used to teach in English. Preferential policies thus involved not simply a transfer among groups but also net losses of financial and human capital to the country as a whole. Other losses, such as disaffection among more than

40 percent of its population who are not Malay, are harder to quantify or even estimate. It is a federal crime to criticize publicly Malaysia's racial policies, so voting with one's feet is the only legal form of protest.

Sectoral Differences

Like preferential policies in other countries, those in Malaysia were labeled "temporary" when initiated. They in fact began with a fifteen-year cut-off date. But, long before that date was reached, preferences for Malays were made a permanent part of the country's constitution. The preferences did not merely persist; they grew stronger in higher education and spread to other sectors of the society.

The dramatic changes in ethnic occupations within the government sector were not matched in the private sector. From 1980 to 1985, for example, the proportion of "professional and technical" workers who were Malays rose by less than one percentage point. If teachers and nurses—both likely to be government employees—are dropped from this category, Chinese professional and technical workers increased by larger numbers than the Malays and so did the Indian professionals.[34] Among private sector doctors, engineers, accountants, architects, and lawyers, the Chinese continued to outnumber the Malays absolutely in 1984, after more than a decade of preferential policies, though in most of these fields the Malay professionals were increasing at a faster rate. Among dentists and veterinary surgeons, even the small Indian minority outnumbered the Malays.[35] Here as in the very different settings of the United States and South Africa, the same economic principle is at work: Non-preferred groups do better in the private sector, where the costs of discrimination are higher, than in the public sector, where discrimination is virtually free.

INDIA

India is not only the world's largest multi-ethnic society but also one of the most socially fragmented, with powerful religious, caste, regional, and ethnic differences cross-cutting the society and expressed from lifestyle differences to bloodshed in the streets. Historically, the difference between a Brahmin and an untouchable has dwarfed intergroup differences in all but the most racist societies in the world. Clashes between Hindus and Moslems in India have produced some of the great bloodbaths in human history, including an estimated half million deaths from mob violence at the time of independence.[36]

There are an estimated 180 languages in India and more than 500 dialects.[37] The language most widely spoken, Hindi, is spoken by only 30 percent of the population, and the next most popular language (Telugu) by only 9 percent.[38] But, despite being a multi-lingual society, India is a nation of predominantly mono-lingual individuals. Less than 10 percent of the population speaks more than one language—including English, which shares with Hindi the status of a national language.[39] Different languages tend to dominate different regions of India—but seldom completely.[40] Being a highly regionalized country with low rates of geographic mobility[41] prevents India from being a Tower of Babel. Nevertheless, minority groups and minority languages are also widespread in the various regions of the subcontinent.

Some have claimed for India the distinction of having had preferential policies longer than any other country, as well as more extensively than any other country. If the definition of preferential policies is limited to *compensatory* preferences for less fortunate groups, this may be so. Preferential policies of this sort began in India early in the twentieth century, during the colonial era, and also appeared in states ruled by Indian princes.[42] However, preferential policies favoring already more fortunate majorities in the United States and South Africa—which is to say, discrimination against minorities—antedated India's preferential policies and similar majority preferences go back for many centuries in many other countries. Compensatory preferences for less fortunate minorities will be covered in Chapter 4. The present focus is on preferential policies favoring demographic or political majorities.

In India, preferential policies for majorities are state or local, while preferential policies for less fortunate minorities (such as untouchables and tribal groups) are national, supplemented by local programs. Independent India's constitution, like that of the United States, contains an amendment prescribing equal treatment by government. However, India's constitution explicitly exempts programs designed to advance untouchables, less fortunate tribal groups, and "other backward classes." This last nebulous and undefined category has provided the legal basis for local majority preferences. Historically, logically, and politically, local majority preferences are derivative from national minority preferences. However, this is not to say that local majority preferences in India are less significant numerically, economically, or socially.

Nationally, untouchables and tribal groups together constitute approximately 20 percent of the population of India. Yet preferential policies cover approximately 50 percent of the population.[43] There are estimated to be roughly 104 million untouchables, 51 million tribal people, and 300 million in "other backward classes." Clearly, the "other backward classes" are in practice not the incidental after-thought that they may have been in the minds of those who wrote India's constitutional exemption from equal-treatment requirements. The same reasoning which equates statistical "under-representation" with "disadvantages,." to be redressed by government, can be applied to majorities as well as minorities—and has been in India, as in other countries. Among the Indian states where this has happened are Assam, Maharashtra, and Andhra Pradesh.

Assam

The state of Assam, in northeastern India, covers an area of more than 30,000 square miles—nearly twice the size of Switzerland. Assam is hilly, rainy, and agricultural, with large forest areas. The literacy rate in 1971 was 29 percent—which was the national average at the time.[44] The Assamese language is the language most widely spoken, but it is only one of many languages in this very ethnically diverse state.[45] Although the ethnic Assamese are Hindus, about one-fourth of the state population is Moslem.[46] Moreover, the principal minority group, the Bengalis, have both Hindu and Moslem communities. Refugees from neighboring Bangladesh—one of the few countries in the world poorer than India—have swelled the Bengali Moslem population in recent years. There are also indigenous hill tribes, who are not considered part of the ethnic Assamese, and have in fact had numerous clashes with the ethnic Assamese.

As in Malaysia, economic development of a modern industrial and commercial sector in Assam has been largely the work of outsiders. In colonial times, the British-owned tea plantations had great difficulties attracting a steady, full-time workforce from among the Assamese, who owned much rich fertile land of their own, and were available only sporadically. The tea plantations attracted ethnic Assamese peasants only during the latter's off season, and relied more on hill tribesmen.[47] They were also forced to import Chinese laborers from as far away as Singapore.[48] These Chinese were paid four or five times the wages paid to the local Assamese.[49] Today, other migrants continue to earn more than the Assamese.[50]

If the importation of Chinese coolies, and their higher pay, suggest that the Assamese were not considered desirable workers, the comments of observers and employers of the Assamese have told much the same story over the years. Just as the British during the colonial era referred to the "indolence and incapacity" of the Assamese, to their "utter want of an industrious, enterprising spirit,"[51] so today many Marwari businessmen refer to their Assamese employees as lethargic, unreliable, untrustworthy, and unwilling to work long hours.[52] A more charitable characterization is that the Assamese are "a leisurely people."[53]

In colonial times, the British imported Bengalis for responsible positions.[54] The Bengalis were a sharp contrast to the Assamese. They were notably successful not only in the colonial bureaucracy, but also in agriculture and the professions. Coming from crowded Bengal, where land was scarce, the Bengalis eagerly seized the abundant idle land in Assam, cleared jungles, and farmed with far more care and energy than the Assamese. By the early twentieth century, an official in a district where the Bengalis had settled declared: "These people have brought in their wake wealth, industry and general prosperity of the whole district."[55]

The Bengalis also seized upon educational opportunities created by the British in India. They became not only trusted administrators in the colonial government but also doctors, lawyers, teachers, journalists, and were well represented in other occupations requiring literacy. By and large, it was the Bengali Hindus who pursued these occupations while the Bengali Moslems became prosperous farmers.

Another migrant group that played a major role in the economic development of Assam were the Marwaris. A business community originating in the western state of

Rajasthan, the Marwaris under British rule migrated all over the Indian subcontinent, beginning as poor traders and eventually ending up as one of the most prosperous groups in the country.[56][57] In Assam, the Marwaris opened up the region to trade and became the dominant group in that trade. Their occupations included merchants, manufacturers, bankers, rice dealers, and innumerable other commercial and industrial roles. They became the premier businessmen of Assam, especially in the large cities. The Marwaris also developed their own separate community organizations: charities, hospitals, schools, newspapers. They spoke Hindi rather than Assamese.[58]

As Assam developed economically, it was the *non*-Assamese who dominated the new sectors. The tribesmen provided the labor force for the tea plantations, and many of them later acquired their own smaller land holdings on which they grew tea. More than half the construction workers in Assam are migrants and most of the local construction workers are tribesmen, not ethnic Assamese.[59] Artisans come from the Punjab. As already noted, Bengalis have historically dominated the professions, government and private, and the Marwaris dominate business, industry, and finance.[60]

The Assamese have largely remained peasant farmers with rich, fertile land, suffering a sense of social status embarrassment rather than poverty.[61] Few Assamese are landless agricultural laborers, like so many people in other parts of India.[62] The Assamese were slow to see a need for education, with the result that the Bengalis were many years ahead of them in making use of educational opportunities and the employment opportunities that followed from that. This in turn meant that the language of education and of government was, for years during the colonial era, Bengali rather than Assamese, presenting a handicap for those Assamese who did eventually want to go to schools or colleges.

Like so many similar groups elsewhere, frustrated in the

competition of the marketplace, the Assamese have turned to politics, to symbolism, and to violence. As early as the 1860s, Assamese nationalists were able to get the colonial authorities to change the language of the schools from Bengali to Assamese.[63] By 1920, the British were attempting to restrict the inflow of migrants into Assam,[64] in response to Assamese pressures, fears, and resentments.

As elsewhere in India, ethnic battles were fought under linguistic labels. The demand was that Assamese be not merely the language of instruction for Assamese students but for all students, not merely the official language of Assam but the *exclusive* language in state government institutions. The Bengali Hindus wanted both Hindi and Assamese to be used, in view of the large numbers of people who spoke each language. But this would have implied equal opportunity in education and employment, and what the Assamese were seeking was the institutionalization of preferential treatment which they already enjoyed in state government employment.[65] This was often rationalized as defensive preferences to forestall "cultural genocide" because of the many advantages of the Bengalis, who would otherwise tend to assimilate the younger generation of educated Assamese.[66]

The battle was not confined to the political arena. Riots broke out in Assam in 1960 and again in 1972 over linguistic issues that were in fact ethnic conflicts. In the mid-1960s, local politicians and college students denounced Marwari businessmen for not hiring enough Assamese employees, and riots and arson erupted against their businesses in Assam. Socialism has also become widely popular among the Assamese, since this would imply confiscating businesses owned by other groups.[67]

In 1972, the demand to make Assamese the exclusive language of the state's universities provoked riots among both the Assamese and the Bengali Hindus, as the authorities vacillated on the language issue. A compromise that would make Assamese the exclusive language of two universities and Bengali the language of one was rejected out of hand by Assamese activists. In a purely linguistic issue, that might have seemed like a reasonable compromise, but as an ethnic issue, the compromise would have represented a complete defeat for the Assamese attempt to institutionalize preferential employment opportunities. Against this background, a decision to let Bengali students answer questions on university examinations in their own language was enough to set off large-scale riots, arson, and looting in a number of towns in Assam. Troops had to be brought in to restore order.[68]

The preferential demands first addressed to government institutions spread into the private sector. The state government asked private industrialists to hire *only* "local" people for jobs below the highest levels. National government installations, which are mandated to hire on a country-wide basis, were also criticized and pressured to hire locals.[69] The national government either evaded the issue as to whether "local" was defined residentially or ethnically or, when specific, defined it non-ethnically in terms of birthplace or residence. But the state government of Assam was much more consistent in meaning ethnic Assamese. The law forbade their saying so explicitly, but they let it be known that no one should misunderstand them. A committee of the state legislature declared:

> In the absence of any clear-cut definition of the term "local people", the Committee has had to base its analysis on place of birth in Assam as being the yardstick of local people. This yardstick is palpably inadequate and misleading and a clear understanding should be there in government and all others concerned in the matter as to what is meant by the term "local people".[70]

In short, employers who wanted to stay on the good side of the state government should hire ethnic Assamese. Local government authorities required *language* information on employees, not simply residence or birthplace.[71]

The consequences of mob violence and political pressures have been varied. Some people have clearly been repelled, in one way or another. In a decade when factory employment in India was increasing by 25 percent, factory employment in Assam declined absolutely—and Assam was the only state to experience a decline. Few licenses for new industrial enterprises in general were issued in Assam, despite a large increase in such licenses in India as a whole.[72] Some of the local tribes have had their territories detached from the state of Assam after pressuring the national government to do so. This pressure has included open rebellion.[73] Whether or how many Bengalis have left Assam is much harder to determine, since there is a large-scale influx of illegal Bengali refugees from Bangladesh.

The government sector of the economy tends especially to hire the locally dominant ethnic group. In Assam, public sector firms hired Assamese at more than twice the rate of private sector firms.[74] Whatever their economic consequences, the preferential policies have been a political success for the Congress party in Assam. Even when the party lost its majority of the popular vote nationally in 1971, it maintained a majority in Assam.[75]

Heightened intergroup tensions have taken their toll. India's 1981 census has had to be postponed in Assam because of local tensions. In 1983, Assamese mobs turned against Bengali Moslems, many of whom are refugees from Bangladesh, and slaughtered more than a thousand defenseless people.[76]

Maharashtra

Historically, there was a state of Bombay as well as a city of Bombay. However, in 1960, the state was divided to create two new states, Gujarat and Maharashtra, with the city of Bombay being the capital of the latter. Many Gujaratis, however, live in Bombay and are prominent among its businessmen.

Bombay has long had a reputation as a cosmopolitan city, being not only a major international port but also a crossroads for people from various parts of India. As far back as 1881, only half the people living in Bombay were Maharashtrians. Yet the variety of its people does not make Bombay a "melting pot." Even in its slums, different streets and paths are occupied by people from a given state, district, or village elsewhere in India.[77]

Historically, it was the "outsiders" who developed the industrial and commercial sector of Bombay—though these outsiders were Indians rather than foreigners.[78] Even the well-to-do local classes were socially and economically eclipsed by the influx of Parsees and others who became traders, importers, industrialists, shipowners, and bankers. The indigenous Maharashtrians long remained outside the industrial and commercial sector, even as workers. There were few businessmen among them.[79] The net result has been that in Bombay, the capital of Maharashtra, the Gujaratis were the largest single group of business managers in 1950, constituting just over half the managers in the companies surveyed.[80] Maharashtrians were not only not hired for managerial positions, but were also regarded as not very good workers, either in skills or in attitude.[81]

Because Maharashtrians have been concentrated in low-level jobs—domestic servants, laborers, factory workers—the higher occupations to which they aspired were largely those within immediate striking distance. These were primarily clerical and other white collar jobs, rather than managerial or professional work. Therefore their primary ethnic conflict was not with the Gujaratis, who were the dominant group in the highest echelons, but with people from southern India, who held many of the office jobs coveted by the Maharashtrians.[82] Indians from the southern regions tended to be better typists, to speak better English, and were considered more diligent and cooperative workers than Maharashtrians.[83]

In politics, however, Maharashtrians have become well represented, especially after the restrictive property qualifications for voting were removed. Although only 12 percent of Bombay's municipal council in 1875, Maharashtrians were 43 percent of the council by 1961—the same as their percentage of Bombay's population in the latter period.[84] Along with the rising political power of the indigenous population came a rising rate of literacy in Bombay—from 16 percent in 1872 to 24 percent in 1931 and 59 percent by 1961. This growing class of educated and semi-educated people has had two major consequences. First, it created a class of Maharashtrians unwilling to take the kinds of jobs traditionally held by their forebears, but now considered beneath them. Their growing literacy also created a mass audience for political propaganda, exploiting the "under-representation" of Maharashtrians in high economic positions. Out of these circumstances there emerged in 1966 a new political movement called Shiv Sena, agitating for preferential quotas for Maharashtrians in Bombay.[85]

The founder and leader of this movement was Bal Thackeray, editor of a local weekly, despite having been a dropout from secondary school at age sixteen.[86] He was, however, extremely clever at appealing to other young, partly educated Maharashtrians. Thackeray first achieved prominence, and rapidly rising circulation for his weekly, by repeated "exposés" of the dominance of "outsiders" in high economic positions in Bombay. One story, for example, claimed that there were only 75 Maharashtrians out of 1,500 business executives in the city.[87] The Shiv Sena movement was created at an outdoor protest rally and its membership has consisted largely of the young—76 percent being not older than thirty[88]—and of Maharashtrians who are the first members of their family to receive schooling.[89] Most are employed on their first or second jobs.[90]

Shiv Sena means "the army of Sivaji"—a regional, seventeenth-century military hero[91]—and the movement operates with paramilitary discipline. It has organized boycotts, run candidates for political office, organized labor union and social service branches, and threatened and carried out violence. The movement has been implicated in violence and murder against both workers and businessmen who are not Maharashtrians.[92] When a boycott of small but popular eating places run by South Indians failed, some of these businesses were destroyed by fire.[93] When an ultimatum for more hiring of Maharashtrians was delivered to an executive of India Oil, it was accompanied by the statement: "You are sitting inside the office, but your oil drums are outside."[94] Thackeray has publicly acknowledged his admiration of Hitler's forcefulness.[95]

The Shiv Sena movement has remained centered in Bombay and its activities largely confined to the state of Maharashtra. It has demanded that 80 percent of the jobs in Bombay be reserved for Maharashtrians. Its followers and supporters now include some Maharashtrian small businessmen,[96] who are struggling to compete with outside groups which have a longer entrepreneurial tradition. Shiv Sena's rallies have drawn as many as 200,000 people.

The dynamics of chauvinism and counter-chauvinism have affected this strident regionalism. A dispute with the neighboring state of Karnataka over which state should encompass a particular border city led to mob violence against Maharashtrians living in Karnataka. Shiv Sena then launched a terrorist campaign against Karnatakins living in Bombay, followed by a one-day strike that paralyzed the city.[97] When a Shiv Sena member murdered a street vendor from southern India, vendors from southern India organized their own Hawker Sena for self-defense.[98] A reported insult to the Moslem religion by Thackeray set off mob violence in Bombay and vicinity in 1984, costing more than two hundred lives and leaving more than 10,000 homeless.[99]

By 1968—just two years after its founding—Shiv Sena won 30 percent of the municipal council seats in Bombay, second only to the nationally dominant Congress party, and far ahead of the many other parties in the city.[100] This was, however, the high-water mark of Shiv Sena's electoral success at the municipal level. Its percentage of seats in the municipal council declined in successive elections in 1973 and 1978, though it remained the principal opposition party in the city.[101] It has failed to elect anyone to the national parliament and has elected few candidates to seats in the Maharashtrian state legislature.[102] However, Shiv Sena's electoral fortunes are no measure of the movement's success, and may in fact reflect the adoption of its preferential treatment goals by elected officials of other parties, both at the municipal and state levels.

Initially cautious about responding to demands for quotas, the Maharashtra state government has progressively increased pressure on private employers to hire Maharashtrians. Because of the national constitution, these pressures took the form of preferences for "local" residents, defined as those who have lived in the state for 15 years or more. These preferences applied at first to low-level government jobs. Over the years, however, preferences spread to higher-level jobs. Moreover, a 1973 directive specified not merely "local" persons but also speakers of the Marathi language—that is, people *ethnically* Maharashtrians. This had national repercussions, including editorial condemnation by the *Times of India,* questions raised in the national parliament, and communications from the central government authorities.[103]

Under this pressure, the state government removed the

linguistic requirement. However, state government forms still required linguistic information on employees[104] and Shiv Sena representatives have made it clear in their confrontations with employers that their definition of a Maharashtrian is *ethnic,* not residential.[105] Few employers are likely to misunderstand what the state authorities want, and the large role of government in the economy makes defiance too costly to be likely.[106] For example, when a company needs more electricity it must seek state approval. As an official of a Bombay textile mill put it: "Once when we applied for power, Government required information from us on the numbers of local persons we employ."[107]

The rise of Maharashtrians to higher-level employment in Bombay has been striking. Maharashtrians were already 64 percent of all employees in higher-level positions in the state and municipal government in 1962, and this rose to 82 percent by 1973. Among high-level employees of the national government in Bombay, the rise was from 19 percent to 29 percent, and among private firms, from 7 percent to 16 percent. Among managers of private companies in Bombay surveyed in 1970, 21 percent of those hired since 1960 spoke Marathi, compared to 12 percent of those hired in the previous decade and *none* among those hired before that.[108]

While these data suggest that preferential policies have been effective, especially in local government employment, there are also other factors to take into account. One is that the rise of Maharashtrians to higher-level occupations began before Shiv Sena or preferential policies by local government, though this rise was faster afterward.[109] Another factor is that the occupational rise of Maharashtrians has followed an extremely rapid increase in education in Maharashtra. Secondary school enrollment in the state rose more than three-fold between 1950 and 1965, as did enrollment at the University of Bombay from the early 1950s to 1971. The local economy has also been expanding, especially in white collar employment.[110]

The chief losers in the rise of Maharashtrians to managerial levels have not been the prosperous and dominant Gujaratis, but people from southern India, who have historically had much more modest shares of managerial positions. Among managers in the private sector hired since 1960, Gujaratis remain the largest group, holding 44 percent of such positions, down from 52 percent among those hired before 1950, though still more than double the percentage for any other group. South Indians—the principal target of nativist hostility—declined from 25 percent to 12 percent.[111]

Preferential policies seem also to have been a political success. Maharashtra in 1971 produced one of the highest proportions of votes for the ruling Congress party—64 percent, compared to 44 percent nationally. The Congress party also found success in the state of Assam, where it also supported preferential policies. In India, as elsewhere, votes reflect more than one issue. But the ruling party seems to think that preferences are politically an asset. Its longer-run economic consequences for the country are another matter.

Andhra Pradesh

The city of Hyderabad was once capital of the state of Hyderabad, which has since disappeared with a reorganization of India's internal boundaries in the 1950s. Instead of being in the southern part of the state of Hyderabad, the city is now in the northern part of the state of Andhra Pradesh, which in turn is in southeastern India. The fifth largest city in India, Hyderabad had a population of more than two and a half million in 1981. The population of the state of Andhra Pradesh is more than fifty-three million people,[112] spread over 107,000 square miles[113]—an area larger than Great Britain. The literacy rate in Andhra Pradesh in 1981 was 30 percent, slightly below the national average of 36 percent.[114]

The language divisions that fragment other states are not as great in Andhra Pradesh, where 86 percent of the people speak the regional language, Telugu.[115] In the city of Hyderabad, however, only 64 percent of the people speak Telugu, though this is still a substantially higher proportion of regional language speakers than in Bombay or in the urban areas of Assam.[116] Nevertheless, despite an absence of linguistic issues, Hyderabad has been the scene of on-going interethnic conflicts—in this case, among people who speak the same language, share many cultural similarities, and even intermarry.[117] Hyderabad illustrates the point that linguistic and other cultural differences need not be the fundamental sources of conflict.

In colonial times, when the city of Hyderabad was part of a princely state of the same name, it did not develop the educational facilities which arose in parts of the Indian subcontinent ruled directly by the British.[118] When Hyderabad was annexed to an independent India in 1948, more than three-quarters of its 22,000 villages lacked even a primary school and, where schools existed, the teachers were often poorly qualified.[119]

When the state reorganization of 1956 combined part of the state of Hyderabad with part of the state of Madras to form a more linguistically homogeneous state of Andhra Pradesh, it combined people who were ethnically similar but who were of very different educational levels, work habits, and economic development.[120] Those from the coastal Andhra region (directly ruled by the British in colonial times) were far more advanced than those from the inland Telangana region, in which the city of Hyderabad is located. No one was more acutely aware of this difference than the residents of Telangana in general and of Hyderabad in particular, for they feared the competition of the Andhras.[121] Telangana politicians were assured of quotas of government positions for themselves, Telangana students were given preferential treatment in the educational institutions of the region, and in the city of Hyderabad ancient preferences for indigenous locals (called *mulkis*) were continued.[122]

Nevertheless, the competition of the Andhras proved to be overwhelming to the Telanganans, both in the public and the private sectors. Andhra farmers began buying up land in Telangana and making it far more productive, through modern methods of agriculture,[123] as the land in Andhra itself had historically been more productive than that in Telangana for the same reason.[124] Literacy was also considerably higher in the Andhra region.[125] Of the thousands of Andhras who migrated to Hyderabad, capital of the state, about one-fourth had completed high school or college—far more than among the natives. Many Andhra businessmen also moved into Hyderabad, along with Andhra government officials transferred from the former capital city of Madras.[126]

Hyderabad developed what was called an "Andhra colony"—visibly more prosperous than the natives, or *mulkis.* By 1961, approximately one-fourth of the population of Hyderabad consisted of migrants, including a net inflow of more than 100,000 from the Andhra region.[127] These Andhra colonies were deeply resented by the *mulkis,* who also opposed the coming of migrants from elsewhere, who were in fact a larger number. Demonstrations featured such slogans as "Non-*mulkis,* go back" and "Hyderabad for Hyderabadis."[128] While there were some claims of discriminatory treatment against *mulkis,* from the beginning there was also a general concession that the Andhra were more efficient workers. A prominent Telanganan leader frankly declared:

> Yes it is true that they are also better qualified for many of the jobs than we are. Maybe they are better qualified but why is merit so important? We can have some inefficiency. That will be necessary if our people are to get jobs. Are we not entitled to jobs just because we are not as qualified?[129]

A rapid increase in educated young people, in both Telangana and Andhra, escalated antagonisms, as both groups competed for government jobs in the state government in Hyderabad. Local preference laws became embroiled in court cases and political agitation.[130] In 1969, a new political movement arose in Hyderabad, demanding that jobs be "safeguarded" for *mulkis.* Riots broke out among university students in Hyderabad and disorders spread to other parts of the state, including looting and arson by Telanganans, with Andhra refugees sent fleeing the region.[131]

After the violence subsided, a new political party was formed, which in 1971 won 10 of the 14 seats in Telangana against the Congress party—even though the Congress party in India as a whole won the largest electoral victory ever in that year.[132] University students, civil servants, and farmers who had sold their land to Andhra farmers were its strongest supporters.[133]

Because the Andhras and Telanganans were of the same race, religion, and language, Telanganan leaders who attempted to create a sense of ethnic solidarity to distinguish themselves from the Andhras were forced to resort to minor differences in lifestyle—a preference for tea rather than coffee, or a different manner of greeting,[134] for example. Nevertheless, the antagonisms generated between the two groups eventually led both to seek to become separate states—with separate sets of government jobs.

In December 1972, Prime Minister Indira Gandhi intervened with a compromise solution which involved a constitutional amendment. It was henceforth allowed that preferential treatment might apply not only in favor of state residents as a whole against "outsiders" but also that such preferences could apply to given districts *within* a state as against other state residents from other districts. Since all parties now had the right to discriminate in their own localities, without separation into new states, separatist movements on both sides subsided.[135]

The social and economic consequence was that both job markets and university admissions areas were fragmented by local preferences throughout the state. The political consequence was that the Congress party retained its ascendancy over the once threatening separatist party in Andhra Pradesh.[136] Private investment in Hyderabad was not inhibited as in Assam—perhaps because the preferential policies in Hyderabad did not apply to private employment but only to the large government sector.

NIGERIA

Nigeria is the most populous nation in Africa and contains about one-fifth of the entire population of the continent. Ethnically, it has no national majority. The Moslem Hausa-Fulani peoples of the north are the largest group, constituting about 30 percent of the population. The next largest are the Yoruba tribe of the southwest and the Ibo tribe of the southeast. Each is a regional majority and altogether these three groups constitute about two-thirds of the population of Nigeria. There are many other smaller tribes as well. While the term "tribe" is used here, as in Nigeria, these are not small bands of people but ethnic groups numbering in the millions.

Like many newly independent, Third World nations, Nigeria is not simply a country conquered by a colonial power but a country *created* by a colonial power. Its very name was coined by an Englishwoman. The disparate African peoples who inhabited the West African regions that the British consolidated into the colony of Nigeria continued to live disparate lives under British rule and emerged into independence not only with substantial differences among themselves but also with substantial mutual suspicions, fears, and animosities as well. In July 1958—a little more than two years before Nigeria became independent on October 1, 1960—the British Colonial Office issued a *Report of the Commission appointed to enquire into the fears of Minorities and the Means of allaying them.* Because every group in Nigeria is a minority in some region of the country, these "minority" concerns were in fact the concerns of all the peoples of the country.

As in some other African nations, the southward sweep of conquering Moslem groups in Nigeria was arrested by the arrival of Europeans who conquered all the contending Africans. Thus, while northern Nigeria is inhabited primarily by Moslem Hausa and Fulani tribes, southern Nigerians tend to be either Christians or followers of various indigenous religions. These simple historical facts have had a complex and profound influence on events in Nigeria after independence.

The Hausa and Fulani peoples of the northern region are often spoken of collectively, in part because the Islamic way of life is considered a more pervasive and unifying influence than their tribal divisions. Moreover, the invading Fulani established an hegemony over the Hausa before the British arrived.[137] One consequence of Moslem control of the northern region was that Christian missionaries were confined to the southern regions of the colony, to avoid offending the Moslem Emirs through whom the British maintained indirect rule in the north.[138] The net result was that education and hospitals, among other features of Western culture, were concentrated among the peoples of southern Nigeria. As in other parts of the world, historic head starts had enduring consequences. As late as 1950, among 160 physicians in Nigeria, 76 were Yorubas, 49 were Ibos, and only one was Hausa-Fulani, even though Hausa-Fulani were (and are) the largest group in the country.[139] In the Nigerian army, an estimated three-quarters of the riflemen were from the northern Hausa-Fulani region but four-fifths of the Nigerian officers commissioned before 1960 came from other regions. As late as 1965, half the officer corps was still Ibo.[140] Even within the northern regional government itself, the northerners were a bare majority (55 percent) of the Nigerians on its professional and technical staff in 1959—and a distinct minority (8 percent) of the total professional and technical staff, which was still dominated by foreigners at that point. In some occupations, such as medical officers, and for the technical staff as a whole, Nigerians from outside the region outnumbered northern Nigerians within the northern Nigerian government.[141]

This predominance of non-northerners in coveted jobs in the north was not confined to a few elite occupations. Although the number of Nigerians appointed to senior administrative positions in the northern region quadrupled between mid-1948 and mid-1952, these did not include even one northern Nigerian assistant district officer.[142] There was also, in the north, a "near-monopoly by Ibos of clerical and semi-skilled jobs in the postal service, banks, and railway."[143] In the private sector as well, southerners moved into the northern towns and cities as traders, merchants, and artisans.[144] Ibos tended to be especially prominent. Most of the factory workers in northern Nigeria around 1960 were southern Nigerians, mostly Ibos.[145] The

Ibos' situation was analogous to that of many other groups from regions less endowed by nature, who were forced to seek outlets for their talents elsewhere. They were historically less prosperous than other groups, who were especially incensed later to see such upstarts surpass them.

Education was a key factor in these disparities. Although the northern region and the northern peoples (who include other groups besides the Hausa-Fulani) constituted more than half of all Nigeria and all Nigerians, the north was a distinct minority in education at all levels. As of 1926, for example, there were 138,249 Nigerian children in primary school, of whom only 5,210 were in northern Nigeria. Of 518 secondary school students, *none* was in the north. A rapid expansion of education in the years leading up to independence resulted in more than 2.3 million primary school children in Nigeria by 1957—but less than 10 percent were northerners. Among more than 28,000 secondary school students, approximately 13 percent were northerners.[146] As of 1959, the north—with 55 percent of the country's population—had only 9 percent of the country's primary school population and 4 percent of its secondary school population.[147]

Much the same story could be told of higher education. As of 1937, according to a scholarly study, "there was only one Northerner in Yaba Higher College; and as late as 1951 the 16 million of the North had produced only one person with a full university degree."[148] Around mid-century, virtually all the Nigerian students in institutions of higher learning overseas, as well as in Nigeria itself, were southern Nigerians.[149] By the academic year 1959–60, northerners were 9 percent of the 1,051 students at the University of Ibadan and, among the much larger number of Nigerians studying abroad, Hausa-Fulani were still only 2 percent as late as 1966.[150] In short, the demographically and politically dominant region of Nigeria was educationally and economically behind the other regions nationally, both in the private economy and in the national government among both civil servants and military officers. Within the northern region itself, southerners played a disproportionate role in the economy and government. One obvious possibility was to use the superior political power of the northerners to attack the superior educational and economic performance of the southerners.

As independence approached, northern political leaders campaigned for "Nigerianization" of the government service, especially at the higher echelons, where expatriates dominated. However, this "Nigerianization" policy quickly turned into an explicitly admitted "Northernization" policy. As early as 1957, the Public Service Commission of the Northern Region declared: "It is the policy of the Regional Government to Northernise the Public Service: if a qualified Northern is available, he is given priority in recruitment; if no qualified Northerner is available, an Expatriate may be recruited or a non-Northerner on contract terms" (as distinguished from becoming a permanent employee).[151] Even this candid statement of a preferential policy did not fully reveal the basic thrust of this policy. As *The Economist* of London put it: "The North, however, is not content merely to replace its expatriate higher administration; it is determined to replace southerners at all levels." To that end, its Institute of Administration ran cram courses to prepare northerners for jobs ranging from district officers to clerks and typists.[152] A scholarly study likewise concluded: "In its actual application, Northernization has been directed much more vigorously against Southern Nigerians than against Expatriates, and it is clear that few Southerners will be allowed to remain long in any conspicuous positions in the service of the Northern Regional Government."[153] Another scholar said: "Expatriates were actually preferred to southerners when no northerner was available."[154]

Strange as it may seem that Africans would prefer Europeans over other Africans, the pattern is completely parallel to that in India's state of Maharashtra, where South Indians were more of a target than the more prosperous Gujaratis, whose higher positions were less accessible. Moreover, the obvious advantages of the Europeans made their success less of a threat to the self-esteem of the Hausa-Fulani than the success of the upstart Ibo. Again, this fits a more general international pattern of modestly successful middleman minorities being hated more virulently than genuinely privileged nobility or multi-millionaires. Asians in Africa have usually faced more hostility than Europeans and have been more badly treated.[155]

Other patterns found internationally are also found in the history of preferential policies in Nigeria. First, the rise of a newly educated class preceded and fueled the drive for preferential policies.[156] Second, the initial scope of preferences widened with time: "Gradually, provisions accumulated excluding southerners from government contracts, retail trade, and ownership of land."[157] The preferences also spread from the northern regional government to the federal government, which gave preferential appointments and promotions to northerners, as well as preferential admission to federal secondary schools and college.[158] Finally there was a "progressive polarization" in Nigeria.[159] Partly this was the result of newspapers and political leaders who kept the various groups "amply supplied with ethnic accusations and suspicions."[160]

Among the signs of political polarization have been the radical disparities in votes received from one state to another by candidates representing different ethnic interests. Tribalism was not this prominent in pre-independence elections between 1923 and 1942—which were also pre-preferential policy elections.[161] But, in the 1979 presidential elections in Nigeria, each of 5 presidential candidates received less than 5 percent of the vote in at least one of the country's 19 states and an absolute majority—ranging from 54 percent to 85 percent—in at least one other state. Nnamdi Azikiwe, for example, received more than 80 percent of the votes in two states and less than one percent in 6 others. Even the winner, Alhaji Shehu Shagari, received less than 10 percent of the vote in 4 states and gained only about one-third of the vote nationally, though going over 70 percent in 3 other states.[162]

The most dramatic examples of polarization, however, did not take place at the ballot boxes but in the streets. The sporadic eruption of tribal mob violence was climaxed by military coups in 1966, led first by a predominantly Ibo group of officers who were later overthrown by a predominantly northern Moslem group of officers. One of the key factors provoking the counter-coup was an announced policy of federalizing regional civil services and the establishing of national norms for all applicants. To the northerners, this meant the return of southern domination and mass pre-emption of coveted jobs.[163] The military coups and accompanying murders were by no means the most violent events in the Nigeria of 1966. Far worse happened as northerners, military and civilian, turned on the Ibos living in their region:

> Northern soldiers chased Ibo troops from their barracks and murdered scores with bayonets. Screaming Moslem mobs descended on the Ibo quarters of every northern city, killing their victims with clubs, poison arrows and shotguns. Tens of thousands of Ibos were murdered in the systematic massacres that followed.[164]

These events provoked a mass exodus of Ibos to their own southern region—and the secession of that region from Nigeria, proclaiming itself the independent nation of Biafra. In the bitter and bloody civil war that followed over the next two and a half years, more than a million people died—some from military action and others from starvation, as the Nigerian government blockaded the Ibo region.[165] Ultimately, the Ibos surrendered. Many expected a bloodbath. However, the long and costly struggle produced a prudent moderation, rather than vengeance, on the part of the victors. Within a relatively short time, Ibos were able to return to their normal pursuits, both in their own region and in Nigeria as a whole.

The country's constitution was altered in an attempt to reduce divisive ethnic appeals. Some of the preferential policies were rescinded[166]—one of the few instances where such policies have been cut back anywhere. However, this has not meant a return to open competition. Instead, there has been a tendency to give something to every group or region, to have federal appointments and university admissions, for example, reflect "the federal character" of Nigeria.[167] Among other things, this means that it is possible for students from some regions to gain admission to a university with substantially lower test scores than students from other regions.[168] But none is systematically excluded.

SRI LANKA

The island nation of Sri Lanka, off the southeast coast of India, began its independence in 1948 with a much more hopeful prognosis for intergroup relations than did Malaysia, India, or Nigeria—indeed, in far more promising circumstances than most Third World countries. As a Sri Lankan scholar described the situation:

> In striking contrast to other parts of South Asia (including Burma), Sri Lanka in 1948 was an oasis of stability, peace and order. The transfer of power was smooth and peaceful, a reflection of the moderate tone of the dominant strand in the country's nationalist movement. More important,

> one saw very little of the divisions and bitterness which were tearing at the recent independence of the South Asian countries. In general, the situation seemed to provide an impressive basis for a solid start in nation-building and national regeneration.[169]

Yet this optimism, shared both by outside observers and by Sri Lankans themselves,[170] proved to be painfully and disastrously mistaken. The worsening of relations between the Sinhalese majority (about 70 percent of the population) and the Tamil minority (about 20 percent) began with preferential policies.

When the British colony of Ceylon became the independent nation of Sri Lanka, the leaders of its Sinhalese and Tamil communities were both committed to peaceful relations between the two groups and both were represented in the government. The Sinhalese and Tamils remained separate communities, with different religions (Buddhism and Hinduism, respectively) and different languages (Sinhala and Tamil), but this had not prevented a largely peaceful coexistence under British rule. As late as 1952, an observer could write:

> In general, relations among these main communities in Ceylon are cordial, unmarred by the sort of friction that exists between Hindus and Moslems in India. Except for one sad episode in 1915, racial riots have been unknown. Religious and racial harmony is present in high degree: Buddhists celebrate Christmas, Christians take part in Wesak illuminations, Buddhists appear in great numbers at Hindu festivals, and so forth.[171]

Both Sinhalese and Tamil elites were English-speaking, educated, and Westernized—and these elites often lived in proximity to each other and apart from the more traditional members of their respective groups. These elites were expected to be a force for mutual accommodation between Sinhalese and Tamils. The Sinhalese majority and the Tamil minority have each had significant internal subdivisions and there are a number of smaller ethnic and religious communities as well. But it was the Sinhalese-Tamil relationship that proved to be crucial—and tragic—for Sri Lanka.

As in so many other Third World countries, different groups in Sri Lanka felt the impact of Western civilization differently and responded to it differently. A succession of colonial rulers began with the Portuguese (1597–1658), continued with the Dutch (1658–1796), and concluded with the British (1796–1948). Each nation's Christian missionaries came to Sri Lanka. The first missionary schools were established under the Portuguese in Colombo and in Jaffna[172]—that is, in both Sinhalese and Tamil areas. However, the missionary schools that were destined to have historic impact were the English-language schools established on the northern tip of the island, the Jaffna peninsula—a heavily Tamil-populated area. The British established schools in the north[173] and so did American missionaries, who established a school that eventually became Jaffna College.[174] The Tamils not only received English-language education first but were also more receptive to education. Living in an arid, less fertile, and less developed part of Ceylon,[175] they saw in education one of their few chances for improvement.[176] The Tamils thus had a head start in Western education—and, as in other places and times, historic head starts had enduring consequences.

Education developed rapidly in Ceylon, mostly through the spread of missionary schools, but it started from a very low level of literacy—only 17 percent in 1881.[177] As late as 1901, only about one-third of the Ceylonese males who were Buddhist or Moslem were literate, as were about one-fourth of the male Hindus and just over half of the Christian males. Female literacy rates were significantly lower among the Christians and far lower among the Buddhists, Moslems, and Hindus.[178] The education that mattered most was education in the English language, which opened up jobs in the British colonial government and in the professions. Few Ceylonese had this but, among those who did, the Tamils outnumbered the Sinhalese, many of whom attended Buddhist schools conducted in the Sinhala language. As of 1921, Ceylonese Tamils also outnumbered the Sinhalese in the legal and medical professions.[179]

A further breakdown of these two groups reveals even more clearly the effects of different exposures to the culture of the West. One segment of the Sinhalese population, those living in the southern highlands of Kandy, remained independent as successive European conquerors took over the remainder of the island. Eventually, the British conquered Kandy as well in 1815, but by then the low-country Sinhalese were ahead of their Kandyan brothers in Westernization. They have remained so ever since. Among the Tamils, those known as "Ceylon Tamils" had roots in Ceylon that went back for centuries. But there was also a large contingent of Tamil immigrants from India and their descendants, all of whom continued to be called "Indian Tamils," generations after their families settled in Ceylon. The Indian Tamils were principally laborers brought over to work on British-owned plantations in southern Ceylon in the nineteenth century. Geographically and socially isolated from the Ceylon Tamils, with their children receiving little or no education, these Indian Tamils were the most poverty-stricken and least educated people on the island.

As of 1921, the percentage of Ceylonese lawyers who were Kandyan Sinhalese was only 4 percent, compared to 46 percent who were low-land Sinhalese, even though the Kandyan Sinhalese population was about half as numerous as that of the low-landers. Ceylon Tamils, who in turn were only about half as numerous as the Kandyans, nevertheless constituted 28 percent of all Ceylonese lawyers. In the medical profession, Ceylon Tamils actually led with 44 percent of all positions, compared to 34 percent held by all Sinhalese (only one-tenth of whom were Kandyan physicians or medical practitioners).[180]

In occupations not requiring a knowledge of English, these groups were very differently represented—but still not in proportion to their respective shares in the population. For example, among coconut plantation owners and supervisors in 1921, 86 percent were low-land Sinhalese, 6 percent were Kandyan Sinhalese, and 3 percent Ceylon Tamils.[181] Virtually all comparisons of Sinhalese and Tamils in high-level positions are, in effect, comparisons of Ceylon Tamils with Sinhalese, largely low-country Sinhalese. Therefore the "over-representation" of Ceylon Tamils (who were about 12 percent of the population in 1921) was in fact even greater than the statistics based on total Tamil population would indicate. In 1942, when Tamils were 19 percent of the population and 32 percent of the students at Ceylon University College, these were virtually all Ceylon Tamils.[182]

The preponderance of Sinhalese among plantation owners and managers highlights one of the contrasts between Sinhalese and Tamils. The Sinhalese live in richer agricultural areas with ample rainfall, and so have options other than jobs in the government and the educated professions, however much such jobs may be coveted. Historically, young Tamils have had to migrate out of their own regions to find jobs in the more prosperous Sinhalese-inhabited regions. Often people left behind in the Tamil regions depended upon remittances from those who were working elsewhere. In short, it was not that the Tamils were the "haves" and the Sinhalese the "have-notes." Rather, the Tamils seized upon education as a way of escaping an unpromising economic situation in their own regions of the island, while the Sinhalese both had other options and, as

Buddhists, were long resistant to Christian missionary schools.

The Tamil head start in education—and its occupational consequences—persisted through the colonial period and into the era of independence. As of 1948, Tamils held one-fourth of all civil service jobs. Since these were Ceylon Tamils, that means that they were "over-represented" by more than double their share of the population. Tamils were also 32 percent of the government's doctors, 40 percent of its engineers, and 46 percent of its accountants. Moreover, the proportion of Tamil doctors, engineers, and accountants in government continued to grow over the next 15 years.[183]

While the political leadership at the time of independence was committed to avoiding ethnic polarization, the whole situation was ripe for a demagogue. Even aside from ethnic issues, the fact that the country's ruling elite was largely an English-speaking group in a country where the vast majority of the people could not understand English meant that official business—including Parliamentary proceedings and court trials—was conducted in a foreign language. The whole lifestyle and cultural allegiance of this group was British rather than Sri Lankan. Add to this the ethnic disparities in education, in the civil service and in the professions, and all the ingredients for a populist crusade were present.

In this setting, the Sinhalese political figure S.W.R.D. Bandaranaike launched a bid for the Prime Ministership in 1956, by demanding a special, preferential place for the Sinhalese language and the Buddhist religion. As has happened so often in countries around the world, this militant extremist grew up remote from the group in whose name he now spoke so stridently. Bandaranaike's family had for generations been devoted to British culture and lived a thoroughly British lifestyle—speaking English rather than Sinhalese, for example, and living in the manner of British aristocrats. Despite Bandaranaike's championing of the Sinhalese language, he grew to adulthood without speaking it. Despite his championing of the Buddhist religion and the Sinhalese peasants, he grew up a Christian aristocrat, having been christened with names taken from his godfather, the British colonial governor. After going away to England to be educated at Oxford, Bandaranaike returned to Sri Lanka, changed language and religion, and became a political crusader for preferential treatment for the Sinhalese masses.[184]

The anomaly of a country's governmental processes being conducted in a foreign language unknown to the great mass of the population gave rise to a demand that Sri Lanka's "own language" be used. But, however politically effective this phrase was, it was logically ambiguous, for the Sinhalese and the Tamils had different languages. More important, the language used—whether English, Sinhalese, or Tamil—would have disparate impact on job opportunities for each group in the government. Within this context, Bandaranaike's attacks on the English-language elite ruling Sri Lanka quickly metamorphosed into a drive for preferential use of the Sinhalese rather than the Tamil language, and was a harbinger of preferential policies in general.

The year 1956 was a turning point in Sri Lanka's history. That year saw not only a stunning political upset victory by Bandaranaike but also a subsequent law making Sinhalese the only official language throughout the island, a government announcement that the country's leading teacher-training college would be reserved for Sinhalese teachers only[185]—and the first of a series of bloody race riots launched by the Sinhalese against the Tamils. An official account of the 1956 riots referred to "many instances of arson and such brutal scenes as men being burnt alive."[186] But, once the political potential of Sinhalese preferences was revealed, political leaders of various parties and movements began a process of trying to outbid each other for

Sinhalese support by demanding extensions and intensifications of preferential policies. Political parties across the ideological spectrum, including Marxist parties, jumped on the bandwagon,[187] in this emotionally charged atmosphere. Tamil protest demonstrations in 1958 were met by Sinhalese mob violence in which hundreds of people—mainly Tamils—were killed, some by being burned alive in their homes.[188]

Bandaranaike, having achieved his goal of becoming Prime Minister through group polarization, attempted to put the issue to rest in 1958 with an accord with the Tamils, compromising on some issues. However, the outcry from the aroused Sinhalese public prevented this accord from being carried out. In 1959, a Sinhalese Buddhist extremist assassinated Bandaranaike for having betrayed the cause.[189] However, the passing of S.W.R.D. Bandaranaike from the political scene did not mean the passing of the group polarization he had aroused or the preferential policies he had spawned. On the contrary, both continued in subsequent administrations, not only when his widow became Prime Minister but also when the political opposition took over the government. Racism could not be turned on and off like a faucet.

Christian missionary schools had long been a sore spot for the Buddhists. In 1960, the government took control of 2,623 private schools "to ensure equality of educational opportunity to all children regardless of race, religion, economic condition or social status" and to provide an education "which is national in its scope, aims and objects and in conformity with the cultural, religious and economic aspirations of the people."[190] In order to complete the changeover of the federal bureaucracy to the Sinhalese language, the government in 1963 began sending Sinhalese government employees to staff their offices in the northern Tamil region in 1963 and in 1964 began compulsory retirement of those Tamil civil servants who could not speak Sinhalese.[191] When one of these Tamil civil servants appealed beyond Sri Lanka's Supreme Court to the Privy Council in London, the Sri Lankan government abolished the right of appeal to the Privy Council. A section of the constitution guaranteeing minority rights was also eliminated in a new constitution.[192]

Polarization worked both ways. As anti-Tamil policies and actions accumulated, as attempts at reason and compromise failed, the moderate Tamil Congress party was superseded by the more militant Federal party, which in 1973 merged with other Tamil groups to form The United Tamil Liberation Front. As attempts to obtain equal treatment at the federal level failed, Tamil demands shifted to more regional autonomy and, finally, Tamil extremists called for a separate nation. When appeals and civil disobedience campaigns failed, armed guerrilla warfare began. But, before things reached that extreme, one final anti-Tamil policy was to drive a generation to desperation. This was a cutback in the number of Tamils allowed to continue on to higher education.

As late as the academic year 1969–70, Tamils constituted 48 percent of all students in engineering and 49 percent in medicine. Over-all, Tamils were only 16 percent of university students—only a modest over-representation compared to the "Ceylon Tamil" percentage in the population. But, as in other countries, the internal distribution of students among fields of study was drastically different between groups, the Sinhalese being heavily concentrated in the liberal arts and the Tamils in the sciences.[193]

The long-standing practice of having students take entrance examinations in English helped conceal the ethnic identity of the individual student, reducing the dangers of favoritism by the examiners. After the controversial new language policies were instituted, however, students began taking examinations in either Sinhalese or Tamil, just as more secondary schools began teaching in these languages.

With ethnic identity now apparent from the language in which university entrance examinations were taken, the way was open for political allegations that Tamil examiners gave higher grades to Tamil students. Despite an investigation which produced no evidence of this, a new policy for "standardization" of examination scores arbitrarily downgraded Tamil scores to enable more Sinhalese students to gain university admission. Protests by university academics of various ethnic backgrounds were ignored.[194] Tamil over-representation declined somewhat but not enough to satisfy the government. New "standardization" procedures were instituted in 1973 on a number of grounds, including compensating for historic differences in science facilities in different regions. In 1974, district quotas were instituted, thereby drastically restricting Tamil admissions in the sciences. Once again, protests by university dons were unavailing.[195] Total Tamil enrollment was not cut as drastically, but the sciences leading to independent professions were now especially crucial, with government employment—a principal outlet for liberal arts graduates—increasingly closed to Tamils and other opportunities still largely lacking in the Tamil regions of the country. University quotas meant, essentially, shutting the door in the face of the younger generation of Tamils.

At about this time, youthful guerrilla movements began in the Tamil regions, committing robberies, arson, assassinations, and other acts of violence. The biggest and most prominent of these were the Liberation Tigers of Tamil Elam, who demanded a separate and independent nation. Guerrilla bases developed in the nearby Tamil areas of India. Once set in motion, these events also acquired a life of their own. Rival guerrilla groups fought each other and terrorized other Tamils. When Sri Lankan army units—overwhelmingly Sinhalese—were sent into Tamil regions to restore order and were ambushed by guerrillas, they sometimes lashed back with indiscriminate attacks on

Tamil civilians. For example, *The New York Times* of August 7, 1983, reported:

> Sri Lankan Army troops pulled 20 civilians off a bus and executed them two weeks ago in retaliation for a Tamil guerrilla attack that killed 13 soldiers a government spokesman confirmed today.[196]

Nor was this an isolated episode. A year later *The Economist* of London reported, "random acts of revenge by soldiers or riot policemen continue."[197]

Meanwhile, Tamils living in Sinhalese regions were in jeopardy when race riots broke out there. Because nearly half the Tamil population lived in areas where the Sinhalese were a majority,[198] this became a major hazard as race riots became more frequent and more lethal. In the 1977 riots, an estimated 150 people were killed and 20,000 made homeless.[199] New outbreaks in 1981 were only a prelude to still worse riots in 1983. Both the 1981 and the 1983 race riots bore the mark of deliberately organized activity by Sinhalese gangs and indifference or complicity by the police and the military—another retrogression compared to their role in the earlier riots of 1958.[200] Sri Lankan President Junius Jayawardene, who shifted position on intergroup issues over the years, declared after the 1981 riots: "I regret that some members of my party have spoken in Parliament and outside words that encourage violence and the murders, rapes and arson that have been committed."[201]

The 1983 riots eclipsed all the previous ones. The official government estimate was 350 dead in the capital city of Colombo alone, but estimates from Tamil sources approached 2,000. Estimates of refugees in Colombo refugee camps alone ranged from 80,000 to 100,000.[202]

Indiscriminate killings of Tamils by the military in the north and by Sinhalese mobs in the south of Sri Lanka were not viewed with indifference in India, with a population of 50 million Tamils and only 25 miles away across the water. By 1985, India had 40,000 Tamil refugees from Sri Lanka.[203] Finally, in August 1987, India landed 50,000 troops in the northern Tamil region to take over the maintenance of order from the Sri Lankan army and police forces, and to disarm the Tamil guerrillas. Although this action restored calm and was welcomed by the Tamil population, the political backlash was savage from those—both Sinhalese and Tamil—who had acquired a vested interest in continued polarization.

Tamil guerrillas protested and resisted being disarmed—a process which cost the Indian army more than 400 lives in the first year. The Sinhalese backlash went beyond reduced political support for the ruling party of President Jayawardene, whose accord with India ratified the troop landing that Sri Lanka could not have prevented in any case. Sinhalese terrorists began their own guerrilla warfare against the government, killing more than 200 supporters of the accord and narrowly missing an assassination attempt on Jayawardene himself.[204]

How effective have the preferential policies in Sri Lanka been? By 1973, the average educational and income levels of the Sinhalese overtook those of the Ceylon Tamils and, of course, greatly exceeded those of the Indian Tamils.[205] Those policies "worked"—but at a high price. Sri Lanka has become almost a textbook example of how even unusually amicable relations between two groups can, within one generation, be turned into implacable hostility, violence, and ultimately civil war, simply by the politicization of race and ethnicity.

IMPLICATIONS

Malaysia, India, Nigeria, and Sri Lanka are by no means the only countries where majorities, or politically dominant groups, vote themselves preferences over minorities who are more economically successful. Very similar stories could be told of Indonesia,[206] Uganda,[207] Fiji,[208] Guyana,[209] Trinidad,[210] Sierra Leone,[211] and much of Eastern Europe in the era of restrictions on Jewish artisans, businessmen, and students.[212]

The implications of majority preferences reach well beyond the countries in which they occur. The widespread economic disparities which lead to demands for preferential policies are difficult or impossible to explain by group discrimination in societies where the more successful group has no power to discriminate against the majority. This is especially obvious in countries where the educational system is wholly controlled by the majority, while a minority is "over-represented" among the students, especially in the more difficult, prestigious, and remunerative fields. This has been true not only of the Chinese in Malaysia, the Tamils in Sri Lanka, and the Jews in pre-war Germany, but also of groups in countries where there has been little or no demand for offsetting preferences. Asian Americans are likewise considerably "over-represented" among college students in the United States, especially at the most prestigious institutions, and particularly in the more demanding and remunerative fields, such as mathematics, science, and engineering.[213] Perhaps the classic case of minority "over-representation" are foreigners, who collectively earned an absolute majority of all Ph.D.s in engineering in the United States in 1987.[214] Clearly, neither Asian Americans nor foreigners have the power to "exclude" the majority of the American population from American colleges and universities, nor to discriminate against them in admissions, choice of fields, or academic success.

In business and the professions as well, minorities have often excelled the majority in competition for the patronage of a majority clientele. This has been commonplace, not only when the minority had a head start over the majority (Indian dentists and Chinese businessmen in Malaysia, Lebanese middlemen and exporters in Sierra Leone, German piano-makers from Australia to America to Russia) but also where the minority arrived as immigrants and displaced an already existing class, as Jewish businessmen did in Argentina, Japanese fishermen in Canada, and Irish politicians in American cities. The keystone of many arguments for preferential policies is that large disparities in "representation" are due to discrimination against the under-represented group is clearly false where the under-represented group is the politically dominant majority, which either controls the institutions in which the disparities occur or forms the bulk of the clientele on whose patronage the minority depends. Group disparities, which are so often discussed in terms of their abstract statistical improbabilities, are empirically and historically commonplace around the world.

CHAPTER FOUR

MINORITY PREFERENCES IN MAJORITY ECONOMIES

Historically, the most recent official preferential policies have been those for minority groups in economies dominated by majority individuals and organizations. Classic examples are untouchables in India and blacks in the United States. However, similar policies have applied to Sephardim in Israel, Central Asians in the Soviet Union, Maoris in New Zealand, and various minority groups in China, Canada, and Britain.

The relatively late appearance of minority preferences, compared to majority preferences, reflects the fact that minority preferences must originate outside the beneficiary group—which is to say, it must await other people's conscience rather than group self-interest. However, that is not to say that group self-interest plays no role, once the preferential principle is accepted by the larger society.

The rationale for preferential policies for minority groups may be compensation for historic wrongs (invasion, enslavement, discrimination) or simply a national effort at redressing "imbalances," however they may have arisen. Even where there is no admission of wrongdoing by the larger society (toward Sephardic Jews in Israel or Central Asians in the U.S.S.R.), efforts may nevertheless be made to moderate or eliminate large group disparities in income, education, or "representation" in desirable or undesirable roles and institutions. India's constitution, for example, allows an exception from the principle of equality of treatment "for the reservation of appointments or posts in favour of any backward class of citizens, which in the opinion of the State, is not adequately represented in the service under the State."[1]

India seems to have been the first nation to have instituted minority preferences. It did so openly and explicitly, for the untouchables, more than half a century ago, under the British colonial government. The constitution of independent India clearly contemplated the continuance of such policies and they have, in fact, both continued and expanded. Minority preferences in the United States are less than half as old as those in independent India, the U.S. policies having evolved largely since the early 1970s. Nevertheless the American experience provides a wealth of information as well.

INDIA

India's "untouchables" are perhaps the world's classic pariah class. Even today—long after untouchability has been officially outlawed—government reports still distinguish "caste Hindus" from "scheduled castes," "Harijans" (children of God, a name given them by Gandhi), and other euphemisms for untouchables. Historically, severe restrictions against touching caste Hindus (and vice versa) were only one of many oppressions against untouchables. In some places, untouchables were not even to let their shadow fall upon a caste Hindu and had to beat drums upon entering a caste Hindu community, to warn others to keep their distance.[2] They could not take water from a well where caste Hindus drank, and in some places still cannot in practice, whatever their legal rights may be. In 1978, an untouchable girl who drew water from a well reserved for caste Hindus had her ears cut off.[3]

Even where they are allowed to take water from the same source, strict caste taboos may still persist. "While taking water from a tap, a Scheduled Caste woman put her water pot on the pot of a caste Hindu woman" is the way an official report describes the beginning of a 1979 riot in which police had to be called in, and in which an untouchable received fatal injuries.[4] The same year, a 15-year-old untouchable boy went to his employer's home to work and drank a cup of coffee that he found there. According to the official report, this "enraged the employer who beat him black and blue" with a stick, until the boy fell unconscious—and later died, having been refused medical treatment by the local doctor.[5] In some cases, police have stood by passively while violence was unleashed against untouchables, and in still other cases the police have themselves initiated the violence, including both murder and rape.[6] Incidents of this sort still occurred in the 1980s. The government regularly collects statistics on officially defined "atrocities" against untouchables. In 1981, these included 493 murders and 1,245 cases of arson, among 14,306 total atrocities.[7] The incidence of such behavior varies greatly from state to state, and especially from rural to urban communities. There are what the government calls "untouchability-prone areas."[8] On the other hand, in some places untouchable students are roommates of caste Hindus in college without incident.[9] A recent survey of 1,155 villages in India found that wells and laundries were accessible to untouchables in just under half the villages. Most temples were not accessible but most hotels, restaurants, and barbers were.[10]

There is not a uniform national pattern, either in behavior or in the definition of an untouchable. Moreover, untouchables are by no means a single homogeneous group, any more than the other castes are. In India, there are literally thousands of local castes, of whom more than 1,000 were placed on the schedule or list of untouchables drawn up by the colonial government for purposes of ameliorative policies. Some groups are considered untouchable in some parts of the country but not in others and some groups of untouchables observe untouchability toward other groups of untouchables.[11] In addition to the various untouchables, the schedule of groups to receive ameliorative benefits included tribal groups deemed backward. Scheduled castes and scheduled tribes are thus often mentioned together and ultimately there developed a government agency called the Commission for the Scheduled Castes and Scheduled Tribes.

Among the social disabilities still suffered by untouchables in some places are restrictions on their "wearing sandals, riding horses, and leading a marriage procession through certain caste-Hindu localities"[12]—in short, dressing or behaving in a way suggesting a dignity above what others are prepared to concede to them. In one wedding procession incident in 1980, 14 untouchables were killed, including 6 burned alive.[13]

The concept and practice of untouchability go back for untold centuries in India. Untouchables performed many tasks that were physically dirty and others that were ritually "unclean" in terms of the tenets of the Hindu religion. Untouchables were—and are—typically the poorest and most powerless group in their respective communities and numerically are nowhere a majority. Whatever the historical origins of their pariah status in their occupations and way of life, that stigma has acquired a life of its own, independent of the occupation or lifestyle of any given individual untouchable. Thus, the most famous of the untouchables, Dr. B. R. Ambedkar, was ousted from a hotel in India when he returned home after receiving his Ph.D. from Columbia University, once it became known that he was an untouchable.[14] To some extent, the caste system followed Indians to other countries, usually varying in its intensity with the distance from India. In nearby Ceylon in the early 1930s, at a time when blacks in the southern United States were supposed to be seated in the back of buses, untouchables were not supposed to be seated at all:

> . . . there was the refusal to concede to *harijans* the right to a seat in buses. Eventually it required government intervention to enforce this right, but attempts to enforce it led to outbreaks of violence in 1930–31, and to a strike of bus drivers and conductors. Previously, *harijans* were expected to stand at the back of the bus, or to sit, or squat, on the floor of the bus even though they were required to pay the normal fare. It took decades before *vellalas* accepted this change, and most of them did so with undisguised reluctance. Discrimination against *harijans* extended to restrictions on entry into cafes and "eating houses," access to village amenities like wells and cemeteries, and on the clothes they wore—their right to wear shoes was a frequent point of contention.[15]

Clearly, if any group can claim to be an historically oppressed minority it is the untouchables. Concern for their plight has come relatively recently in history, and has been by no means wholly humanitarian in origin. At one time, there was a question as to whether untouchables could be considered Hindus at all,[16] since some of their occupations involved making products from animals slaughtered in violation of Hindu tenets. But the struggle for independence in India raised the more pragmatic question of the relative balance of power between Hindus and Moslems after independence. Hindu leaders of the independence movement therefore chose to count the untouchables as part of the Hindu population. Untouchable leader Dr. B. R. Ambedkar maneuvered to gain whatever concessions he could for his people under these circumstances and Mahatma Gandhi took up the untouchable cause as a moral issue.

This new-found interest in the untouchables manifested itself in a number of ways, from legal rights—largely ineffective—to access to schools, wells, and roads, to preferences and quotas in education and government jobs for "backward classes" in general. As early as 1928, Dr. B. R. Ambedkar appeared before an official commission to ask for reserved seats for untouchables in legislative bodies, among other communal preferences. But, when the British granted a separate electorate to the untouchables in 1932, Gandhi vowed to fast unto death unless this policy was revoked.

Fearing for the safety of untouchables all over India if Gandhi were to die as a result of his fast, Ambedkar negotiated a compromise agreement under which untouchables would be part of the general electorate but would still have reserved legislative seats. In legend, however, this has sometimes been represented as Gandhi's fast against the principle of untouchability,[17] when in fact it was an effort to keep the Hindu vote from being fragmented, which might have given political control of India to the Moslems.

In the wake of this episode, which produced heightened national awareness of the general problems of untouchability, efforts to ameliorate the condition of the untouchables proliferated—public accommodation laws in some states, including the right to enter Hindu temples, and government jobs set aside for untouchables in other states.[18] Over the years, especially after Indian independence in 1947, preferential programs for untouchables have included land redistribution programs as well as a growing number of educational benefits and job reservations in government at many levels.

Education

Education has long been the major focus of the Indian government's programs for the advancement of untouchables. Of the first 720 million rupees spent on them over the years, more than half—422 million rupees—went for education.[19] The success of the program cannot be measured, however, by such input variables as money spent or, as it often is, by the number of untouchables participating. The actual educational outcomes must also be taken into account.

In education, as in other areas, a sharp distinction must be made between the official availability of benefits and the practical ability of different individuals and groups to make use of them. Even for the primary grades of school, provided free by the government, the small sums of money required for books and supplies can strain the family finances of poverty-stricken untouchables. Like other rural people around the world, the untouchables may also need the labor of school-age children to contribute to the support of the family. Secondary schools for rural children are sufficiently scarce in India—where most of the population remains illiterate—that rural students might have to commute and pay for boarding.[20] Therefore, like other "free" benefits which are in practice available only to those who can supplement them, education in India is not a practical possibility for all those who are officially eligible, or even for all those who have preferences and quotas instituted on their behalf. This is especially so in higher education, where the supplements to be supplied include many years of prior education. There is also an understandable political tendency to stretch a given sum of money to cover numerous beneficiaries, so that each is inadequately funded—again favoring the more fortunate, who alone may be able to afford the necessary supplement. A study of special scholarships for untouchables in higher education concluded:

> The scholarship money . . . can hardly be expected to induce the really poor to go in for higher education and, if one does go in for it, to continue till he completes the course. Only those who have some other sources to rely on can avail of these scholarships. A few respondents were frank enough to admit that this money provides them with pocket money while their parents bear the major portion of the educational expenditure.[21]

Unused reservations or quotas have been common, and are especially striking at the university or post-graduate level. A 1977–78 survey showed that less than half the university places reserved for members of the scheduled castes or scheduled tribes were in fact filled.[22] A 1969 survey of 42 medical and engineering schools in India showed that scheduled caste students filled much less than half of the 11 percent of all places reserved for them.[23] A later survey of medical schools in 1979–80 and in 1980–81 showed that only 23 out of 77 institutions had full utilization of their quotas for scheduled caste and scheduled tribe students while 10 did not have a single student in either category.[24]

Under-utilization of benefits in fact extends well beyond education to housing subsidies, health programs, maternity and other benefits—so much so that governmental expenditures on these programs have repeatedly fallen short of the funds available.[25] Government jobs reserved for scheduled castes and scheduled tribes likewise often are not all taken, due to a lack of qualified candidates.[26] In their very different ways, these facts all reflect the same need for complementary inputs—whether money or educational performance or job skills—as a prerequisite for taking advantage of the benefits reserved for particular groups.

The failure of students from untouchable backgrounds to fill the available educational openings has been by no means due to a rigid adherence to entrance standards by the institutions concerned. In the Bombay medical schools, for example, lower standards are officially prescribed for untouchables.[27] Even so, in 1974, 40 percent of the untouchable candidates passed the qualifying examination only on the second attempt and another 20 percent only on the third attempt, compared to 97 percent of the non-preferred candidates who passed on their first attempt.[28] By 1978, a new system was used, and in this system the vast majority of all categories of candidates passed.[29] Clearly, the standards were being brought down to the students, rather than raising the students to the standards.

At a medical college in the state of Madhya Pradesh, when the scheduled caste and scheduled tribe candidates "failed to attain even the barest minimum of 35 percent, the qualifying requirement was pushed down to a meager 15 percent so that reserved seats could be filled up."[30] Six highly selective engineering schools in India likewise lowered their admissions requirements for scheduled caste and scheduled tribe students. Normally they select about 1,200 students from among 30,000 who take their joint nationwide examination. Although the normal range of scores of those admitted is from 70 percent to 90 percent on the examination, scheduled caste or scheduled tribe students with scores as low as 10 percent were admitted. Even so, the quota of 54 was never filled, though a high of 42 such students was admitted in 1977. Of 106 preferentially admitted students over a six-year period, only 15 were able to maintain the minimum grade average needed to continue in school—and none of these 15 kept up with the schedule appropriate for a student with his own number of years in attendance.[31]

The need for complementary resources is demonstrated by the fact that, among those who do use the quotas, the more prosperous of the scheduled castes use a disproportionate share.[32] For example, the Chamars of Maharashtra are among the most prosperous of the scheduled castes in that state. They are 17 percent of that state's population and 35 percent of the medical students.[33] In the state of Haryana, only 18 of the 37 scheduled castes officially entitled to preferential scholarships actually received any and one caste—the Chamars—received 65 percent of these scholarships at the graduate level and 80 percent at the undergraduate level.[34] Similar patterns of large disparities within the preferred groups have been found in other parts of India and for scheduled tribes as well as scheduled castes.[35]

The academic performance of scheduled caste students has been substandard in a number of ways. In general, they attend inferior and less prestigious universities and, within these institutions, are concentrated in courses that do not lead to remunerative or high-status occupations.[36] Even so, only 8 percent of scheduled caste and scheduled tribe students received their degrees in the prescribed four years and 85 percent left college without a degree. Moreover, even those few who graduated tended to receive low grades.[37]

At the Bombay medical schools, untouchable students entered nearly three years older than the other students, suggesting a slower pace in finishing college.[38] They entered with generally lower grades, fewer courses in higher mathematics and lower performance even in elementary mathematics, as well as in general science and in English—the language in which students are taught at the Bombay medical colleges.[39]

Against this background, it is hardly surprising that only 22 percent of the untouchable students finished medical school on time, compared to 78 percent of students who entered without preferences.[40] Similar patterns are found among untouchable students studying engineering in Bombay. At Nehru Medical College in Raipur, the results were still worse. Over a period of a decade, 42 untouchable students entered but only 4 completed the medical college within four and a half years and only 23 within eight years.[41] A study of second-year college students at 10 Bombay colleges found that no more than one-fourth of the scheduled caste students passed the examinations required to advance to the third year, during a three-year period surveyed.[42]

The unfilled quotas and high attrition rates among untouchable students are especially (and tragically) ironic in view of the violent backlash against the preferential policies—and against the untouchables. In the state of Gujarat, for example, less than 5 percent of the medical school places reserved for untouchables over a period of five years were actually filled.[43] Yet bloody riots have broken out again and again in Gujarat over medical school preferences for untouchables. In 1981, 42 people died in extensive riots—over 7 places reserved for untouchables.[44]

For India, as a whole, violence against untouchables has been generally rising over the years, amid generally adverse reactions against preferential policies.[45] So are other forms of intergroup violence. In 1976 there were 169 incidents of intergroup violence, with 39 people killed. By 1980, there were 421 incidents of intergroup violence, with 372 people killed.[46] Not all of these began over educational issues, and even some that did were fueled by other issues as well. Gujarat was again the scene of one of the more widespread and prolonged of these intergroup outbursts of violence. A plan to increase the reserved places for "other backward classes" in the medical and engineering schools of Gujarat in 1985 led to months of rioting in various parts of the state, with the estimated deaths exceeding 200 people.[47] Widespread riots have been provoked, not only where substantive benefits were at issue, but also where purely symbolic benefits were involved. A decision to rename the Marathwada University for the late untouchable leader, Dr. B. R. Ambedkar, set off riots in 1978 that spread to more than 300 villages, with 1,725 homes destroyed.[48] Several people lost their lives over this purely symbolic issue.[49]

Government

Preferential policies within government include reserved seats in the lower houses of both the national and state legislatures and preferential employment opportunities in the civil service. These reservations were originally scheduled to expire in ten years, but in 1959 they were extended for another ten years. In 1969 they were again extended for another ten years and in 1980 for yet another decade.[50] Reserved legislative seats, like other preferential benefits, tend to go disproportionately to those already more fortunate. Those untouchables serving in India's lower house of parliament are generally less representative of their constituency—in education, occupation, or urbanization—than other members of parliament *vis-à-vis* their own respective constituencies. Nor are the various untouchable sub-castes evenly represented among the untouchable political elite. In the state of Andhra Pradesh, for example, it was found that only 5 of the 65 untouchable sub-castes were represented among this elite.[51] In the state of Rajasthan, 16 of the 28 state legislators holding seats reserved for untouchables had acquired certificates of untouchability by being adopted.[52] The adoption strategy has also been used by students to gain admission to medical schools and engineering schools.[53]

India's national government has reserved jobs for members of the scheduled castes since 1943 and for members of the scheduled tribes since 1950. The percentage of jobs reserved has increased slightly at the national level and state governments have instituted similar job reservations.[54] Official preferences take various forms, from simple reservations or quotas to waivers of some requirements that other job applicants must meet, to subsidies for travel.[55] Untouchables are most represented in the lowest level of government employment—as sweepers and in other tasks characterized as "menial." They are successively less well represented in clerical, lower administrative, and higher administrative positions. However, their share of the latter three kinds of occupations has increased substantially over the years, though only at the lowest level does their representation approximate their share of the population.[56]

By and large, whether at the state or the national level, the jobs actually held by officially preferred groups have tended to fall short of those reserved for them.[57] In obtaining jobs, as in education and reserved seats, the benefits have favored those already more fortunate. A massive study of preferential policies in India reports "a severe clustering" of "some of the larger and more advanced groups" of untouchables in the jobs reserved for scheduled caste members.[58] In the state of Andhra Pradesh, where 37 percent of the untouchables are Malas, more than half of all fellowships awarded to untouchable students went to Malas. A slightly larger group of untouchables, the Madiga, constituting 44 percent of the untouchable population of the state, trailed far behind the Malas in government jobs, all the way up to the highest echelons.[59]

Preferences have spread from the hiring stage to the promotions stage after 1957 at the national level and state governments have subsequently followed suit. The preferences took the form of both quota reservations and of differential weighting of performance recommendations.[60] The backlash from non-preferred individuals has been especially strong on this issue. The bulk of litigation over reserved jobs has been over promotions.[61] The backlash has also taken the form of supervisors' deliberately neglecting to impart their knowledge to untouchable subordinates, for fear of having them preferentially promoted to—or above—the supervisor's own level.[62]

Land disputes have been one of the major sources of violence against untouchables. Often squatters on government land or on land declared "surplus" by the government launch violence against untouchables who receive such land under government auspices.[63] In one case which occurred only 15 miles from Delhi, untouchables whose right to the land awarded them by the government had been upheld by the High Court were harassed by attackers who set their hay stacks on fire, held untouchable women as hostages, and blocked sales of essential commodities to the untouchable.[64]

THE UNITED STATES

Preferential policies have seldom been explicitly legislated in the United States. Most such policies are the product of administrative regulations or judicial rulings, as well as privately initiated group preferences in industry, the academic world, and other sectors. Thus, unlike preferential policies in some other countries—commencing on a specific date for specific benefits in specific sectors—group preferences in the United States have emerged gradually and unevenly, and not always openly. Both the constitutional mandate of "equal protection of the laws" and the provisions of the Civil Rights Act of 1964 require nondiscrimination, so that many group preferences in the United States were initiated and defended as specific remedial responses to specific discrimination, rather than as policies justified in their own right.

While hard and fast dates are more difficult to assign for the beginning of preferential policies in the United States, one clear turning point was the creation of the Office of Federal Contract Compliance by President Lyndon Johnson's Executive Order in 1965. Its role was to ensure that all private enterprises doing work for the federal government complied with "non-discrimination" requirements—as the OFCC would define it for them. Because many large businesses sell to, or contract to do work for, the federal government, a substantial portion of the American economy became subject to "guidelines" never voted on by elected officials but having virtually the effect of law nevertheless.

Over the period from May 1968 to December 1971, the guidelines evolved from requiring "goals and timetables for the prompt achievement of full and equal employment opportunity" to a requirement that employers eliminate group "under-utilization," defined as "having fewer minorities or women in a particular job classification than would reasonably be expected from their availability."[65] In short, statistical representation became the litmus test of "discrimination" with results *ex post* being equated with opportunity *ex ante.* Specific government-designated groups were now entitled to employment (and other benefits) on the basis of the government's definition of their quantitative "availability" and the government's assessment of their qualifications, rather than the test of the marketplace. The federal guidelines of December 1971 can be said to mark an unmistakable set of preferential policies, toward which earlier guidelines were drifting. These group preferences that emerged administratively and judicially went counter to the major legislation on the subject, the Civil Rights Act of 1964.

In the lengthy debates leading up to passage of the Civil Rights Act of 1964, the controversial concept of group preferences was raised again and again, usually by opponents seeking to discredit the legislation, and was emphatically repudiated again and again by the bill's supporters.[66] This repudiation of preferential policies found its way into the language of this key civil rights statute, which stated that an employer was *not* required "to grant preferential treatment to any individual or group on account of any imbalance which may exist" with respect to the numbers of employees in such groups "in comparison with the total number or percentage of persons of such race, color, religion, sex, or national origin in any community, State, section or other area."[67] Accordingly, administrative regulations and judicial rulings have not imposed a balance in group representation as legally required or desirable in itself, but rather have treated statistical *imbalance* and "under-utilization" as prima facie evidence of discrimination, whose correction is then to be in numerical terms tending toward a more even group "representation."

Although these round-about methods of creating group preferences might seem to be only formally different from what exists in other countries under more straightforward labels, the U.S. Supreme Court has been sufficiently inconsistent in upholding group preferences to leave the issue somewhat more unsettled than it is elsewhere. For example, in 1978 the Supreme Court struck down a state medical school quota for minority students[68] but in 1979—with the same 9 Justices on the Court—upheld a private corporation's minority quota for a training program.[69] In 1980, the Supreme Court upheld a federal government program setting aside a percentage of its construction contracts for minority businessmen[70] but in 1989 it overturned a state program setting aside a percentage of its contractors' subcontracting for minority businessmen.[71] These and other apparent inconsistencies may reflect conscientiousness about the fine legal distinctions made in the particular cases before the Supreme Court. But, as astonished and often bitter dissents by outvoted Supreme Court Justices in these cases suggest, the inconsistencies may simply represent the Court's agonizing vacillations as it seeks to uphold the Constitutional requirement of equal treatment (for which the American constitution provides no exception, unlike the constitution of India), without destroying preferential programs widely believed, among intellectuals at least, to be essential to the advancement of disadvantaged groups.

Whatever the reasons, preferential policies in the United States are not as clearly and solidly established as in some other countries. Nevertheless, these group preferences have by and large not only persisted but also expanded—from the government to government contractors and recipients of governmental money in various forms. Large private sector organizations have also established such policies on their own.

It would be difficult, if not impossible, to understand the historical evolution of preferential policies in the United States without understanding how its general rules and beliefs evolved from observing the special case of black Americans. Largely as a result of the previous set of preferential policies—for the benefit of whites under the "Jim Crow" laws in the south—there were whole institutions, such as particular colleges and universities, where no black person had ever been admitted, whole occupations in government where no black had ever been employed, whole communities where restrictive covenants prevented blacks from buying a house. As court decisions and statutory laws, supported by changing public opinion after World War II, began here and there to erode and undermine this pervasive system of racial discrimination, some institutions found it expedient to admit or to hire one or a few token blacks to defuse the growing criticism and relieve the mounting pressures. Increasingly, these tactics became transparent to everyone and the trivial numbers involved became a subject of derision.

The correlation between trivial numbers and racial discrimination was widely apparent, just as the whole history of blacks was clearly marked by oppression and injustice. The converse was often assumed—that non-discrimination would mean an even representation in institutions, sectors, and levels of the society, equal performance in education, and equal rewards such as average incomes as between groups. Moreover, these beliefs (and the principles and policies derived from them) were successively extended from blacks to other groups whose history and current circumstances diverged further and further from those of blacks. Wherever Hispanics, American Indians, Asians, women, or the elderly were "under-represented," the presumption was discrimination and the accused employer or institution bore the burden of disproving that presumption.

Education

In the United States, as in India, Nigeria, Sri Lanka, and other countries, attention has tended to focus on higher education and on the statistical "representation" of different groups at the college and university level. The qualitative dimensions of their actual performance in higher education has received relatively little attention. Relatively little attention has also been paid to the qualifications of the pool of minority group students that colleges, universities, and engineering schools can draw upon to achieve statistical "balance."

Although Asian Americans are often included among "minority" students, their academic qualifications are radically different from the qualifications of black, Mexican American, Puerto Rican, or American Indian students. For example, although twice as many black as Asian students took the nationwide Scholastic Aptitude Test in 1983, approximately fifteen times as many Asian students scored in the 700s (out of a possible 800) on the mathematics half of the SAT. The percentage of Asians who scored in the 700s in math was also more than six times as high as the percentage of American Indians and more than ten times as high as among Mexican Americans—as well as more than double the percentage among whites.[72] In short, as in other countries, intergroup performance disparities are huge. This is especially so at the extremes—at the kind of performance level common only at a few dozen top-level colleges, universities, and engineering schools. Only eleven engineering schools, for example, have average math SATs in the 700s.[73] Again, just as public attention tends to be focused on higher education, so the attention to and pressures for group "representation" tend to be greatest at the most highly rated and prestigious institutions. It is precisely here that the available pools of students from different groups vary most.

There are dozens of American colleges and universities where the median combined verbal SAT score and mathematics SAT score total 1200 or above.[74] As of 1983, there were less than 600 black students in the entire United States with combined SAT scores of 1200.[75] This meant that, despite widespread attempts to get a black student "representation" comparable to the black percentage of the population (about 11 percent), there were not enough black students in the entire country for the Ivy League alone to have such a "representation" *without going beyond this pool*—even if the entire pool went to the 8 Ivy League colleges.

Clearly, with dozens of top-tier institutions across the country competing for these and other black students, there was no realistic hope of approaching a proportionate "representation" of black students in these institutions without a widespread lowering of admissions standards for them. But, just as American preferential policies are seldom called preferential policies, so a lowering of admissions standards in American institutions has almost never been called a lowering of admissions standards. Rather, "traditional" or "conventional" standards are either disparaged in general or dismissed as "irrelevant" to selecting students from a special background. Sometimes a claim is made that conventional test scores have a "cultural bias" that causes them to be either generally less predictive of the college performance of "disadvantaged" students or, more specifically, to predict a lower performance than they in fact turn out to have.

The often reiterated belief that standardized tests predict a lower subsequent college performance level than in fact occurs with black students has somehow survived innumerable empirical studies which show the *utter falsity* of this claim.[76] There is, in fact, a tendency for test scores to predict a somewhat higher college performance than black students actually achieve.[77] In general, test scores are more accurate predictors than high school grades for blacks, though the reverse is true for whites and Asians.[78] Whether the tenacity with which the belief is held that test scores are less predictive for blacks reflects simply a "will to believe" or a pragmatic need to avoid admitting that admissions standards have been lowered to obtain statistical "representation," this belief simply does not fit the empirical facts. More important, the actual consequences of admitting blacks to institutions where they do not meet the usual admissions standards have been educationally disastrous for those students.

At the University of California at Berkeley, for example, where the entering freshman class has been described as "wonderfully diverse" because "the class closely reflects the actual ethnic distribution of California high school students,"[79] more than 70 percent of black students *fail to graduate.* Tragic as this is, it is hardly surprising, given the admissions patterns. Of 312 black students entering Berkeley in 1987, all were admitted under "affirmative action" criteria rather than by meeting the standard academic criteria. So were 480 out of 507 Hispanic students.[80] In 1986, the median SAT scores for black students at Berkeley was 952, for Mexican Americans 1014, for American Indians

1082, and for Asian Americans 1254. The university's average SAT is 1181.[81]

Despite the wide variations in test scores among these groups of Berkeley students, each group's median SAT is *above the national average.* In short, the black students who failed to make it to graduation at Berkeley were perfectly capable of graduating from an average American college. Their failure was due to their being mismatched with Berkeley. This pattern is neither new nor peculiar to Berkeley.[82] It is the logical consequence of seeking statistical "representation." Such disasters have not been confined to top-tier schools, however. More than 70 percent of the black students at San Jose State University likewise fail to survive to graduation.[83]

Once the process of mismatching begins at the top-level institutions, the second-tier institutions find that the minority students who meet their normal standards of admissions have been siphoned off and so must take minority students whose qualifications are more appropriate for lower-ranked institutions. Once begun at the top, the mismatching process continues down the line, for institutions with conspicuous "under-representation" of minority students face consequences ranging from embarrassing inferences of racism to jeopardizing federal financial support, which runs into many millions of dollars, even at "private" colleges and universities.

Much the same pattern can be found at post-graduate institutions. Among leading law schools in the 1970s, a 600 score on the Law School Aptitude Test and a 3.25 college grade point average were considered essential prerequisites for effective performance. In 1976 there were only 39 black students in the entire United States who met these requirements.[84] Yet by then many leading law schools had special minority programs that brought in large numbers of black students under "special" admissions standards. A study of 10 leading law schools showed that the average grade of their black students was at the 8th percentile.[85]

Intergroup differences persist through to the Ph.D. level. While 20 percent of all doctorates earned by Asian Americans were in mathematics and the physical sciences, blacks received only 3 percent of their Ph.D.s in those fields, American Indians received 6 percent of their Ph.D.s in mathematics and the physical sciences, Puerto Ricans 7 percent, and Mexican Americans just over 3 percent.[86] At the other extreme, more than half the black doctorates were in education, as were 38 percent of the doctorates of American Indians, 46 percent of the doctorates of Puerto Ricans, 41 percent of the doctorates of Mexican Americans—but only 11 percent of the doctorates of Asian Americans.[87] Even where Ph.D.s were in the same general area, such as the social sciences, their internal distribution differed sharply—Asian Americans receiving twice as many Ph.D.s in economics as blacks and indeed more Ph.D.s in economics, econometrics, and statistics than all four other minorities combined.[88]

Over-all, at both the under-graduate and the post-graduate level, blacks, Puerto Ricans, Mexican Americans, and American Indians lag educationally, whether measured by test scores, attrition rates, or the difficulty (and remuneration) of the fields of specialization chosen. Despite sweeping denials that standards are being lowered for the sake of statistical representation of groups, the general patterns are very similar to what is found in countries where preferential policies are more openly acknowledged, such as India, Malaysia, or Sri Lanka.

Another characteristic that American preferential programs share with those in other countries is a backlash among non-preferred people. Racial incidents and general expressions of hostility toward preferred minorities—seldom toward Asians—have occurred on campuses across the United States. These have yet to approach the magnitude of violence found in India, for example. This may be due to cultural differences between the two countries—or to the fact that the preferential programs in India have been going on much longer and have had time to build up more resentments.

Income and Employment

Black Americans, the initial focus of preferential policies and still widely regarded as having the strongest case for such policies, began their history as a free people almost incalculably far behind the general population in economic as well as educational terms. Largely lacking not only job skills but even the experience of functioning independently in the economy and society, blacks had an enormous gap to overcome, in the face of growing official preferences for whites in the South, where the great majority of the black population lived.

Even under these conditions, however, blacks began a slow economic advancement, both absolutely and relative to whites. Despite organized cartels of white landowners who openly combined to restrict the earnings of blacks and their discretion as share-croppers in the post–Civil War years, the incomes of blacks in the South tended to rise at a faster percentage rate than the income of whites during the period from the end of the Civil War until the turn of the century.[89] Moreover, the discretion accorded black share-croppers expanded, more blacks became fixed-rent payers instead of share-croppers, and a few became landowners—all this to the accompaniment of bitter recriminations among white landowners as their cartels failed as decisively as later organized attempts to keep blacks out of Harlem would fail. The proportion of the black population working as unskilled workers and domestic servants tended to decline over the early decades.[90] As late as 1940, however, the annual earnings of black males were only 42 percent of what white males earned. The proportion climbed to 57 percent by 1950, with the younger black males (25–34 years old) earning 62 percent of what their white counterparts earned, at that time, foreshadowing a continued rise as this younger generation began to replace their elders in the labor force.[91] This was the situation at mid-century, on the eve of "the civil rights revolution" which produced legislation and policies mandating first "equal opportunity" and then "affirmative action."

These pre-existing trends continued under the new policies, which were often credited with economic improvements that occurred in the wake of these policies. It is an often-cited statistic that the number of blacks in professional and other high-level occupations increased significantly in the years following passage of the Civil Rights Act of 1964, but it is an almost totally ignored fact that the number of blacks in such occupations increased even more rapidly in the years *preceding* passage of the Civil Rights Act of 1964.[92]

Because blacks were also receiving more (and often better) education compared to the earlier decades of the twentieth century, and were migrating massively out of the low-income South, powerful factors other than federal policy went into raising black incomes and occupations. Some statistical studies which attempted to sort out these various factors concluded that migration was a significant reason for the rise of black incomes relative to that of whites between 1940 and 1970, with enforcement of federal policy being either negligible or even negative in its effect.[93] The largest gains in black wages relative to those of whites between 1960 and 1970 occurred in private sector industries *less* regulated by government and *less* likely to be government contractors.[94]

Black males with more education and more job experience have advanced in income, both absolutely and relative to whites, while black males with less education and less job experience have *retrogressed* relative to whites over the same span of years.[95] In short, the gains have gone to those already more fortunate, as with preferential policies in other countries. The actual retrogression of less fortunate blacks is also in keeping with what happened among the untouchables in India or the Malays in Malaysia. Similarly stagnation, despite massive government programs for their advancement, has been found among the Maoris in New Zealand.[96]

Part of the pattern among black Americans may reflect the greater availability of welfare state benefits, which would compete effectively with labor market alternatives at the lower socioeconomic levels. It may also reflect employers' greater reluctance to hire black workers whose lower skills or shorter track record in the job markets make them more risky to hire. The same risk applies to white workers with little skill or experience, but firing or failing to promote white workers of this sort creates no such legal liability to discrimination charges based on statistics.

The history of other American ethnic groups shows a somewhat similar pattern. Chinese Americans, Japanese Americans, Mexican Americans, and Puerto Ricans living on the U.S. mainland also advanced economically over the years, both absolutely and relative to the general population. Even before preferential policies began with the "goals and timetables" of 1971, the Chinese and Japanese had already exceeded the national average in family income.[97] Ironically, Puerto Ricans as a group have actually fallen further behind during the era of preferential policies,[98] though Mexican Americans have continued to close the gap slightly.[99] Because Puerto Ricans are American citizens by birth, and have migrated to the U.S. mainland largely during the era of a growing welfare state (on the island as well as the mainland), this lends weight to the possibility that the welfare state may itself be a negative factor in the upward mobility of the underclass. Mexican Americans, many of them illegal immigrants or having illegal immigrants in their family, have tended to avoid government programs. The contrast between their continued rise and the relative retrogression of their fellow-Hispanics, the Puerto Ricans, also lends weight to the possibility that the welfare state has negative effects on income at the lower end of the socioeconomic scale.

Whatever the effect of the welfare state on lower-level workers, it is higher-level workers who have advanced most under preferential policies. Black couples in which both husband and wife are college-educated overtook white couples of the same description back in the early 1970s and continued to at least hold their own into the 1980s.[100] Part of the prosperity of middle-class blacks comes from administering government programs. More than half of the increase in black professional, managerial, and technical employment between 1960 and 1979 occurred in the public sector, with employment in social welfare programs accounting for approximately half of that increase.[101]

IMPLICATIONS

In the highly disparate settings of India and the United States, broadly similar patterns of results have followed preferential policies. In education, preferential admissions policies have led to high attrition rates and substandard performances for those preferred students (whether untouchables or blacks) who survived to graduate. As with other groups with substandard educational performances in other countries, untouchables in India and black, Hispanic, and American Indian students in the United States have tended also to concentrate in less difficult subjects which lead to less remunerative careers. This pattern has already been noted in Chapter 3 as applying to the Sinhalese in Sri Lanka and the Malays in Malaysia. In Israel as well, Jews of North African and Middle Eastern origin not only average a smaller quantity of education than do Jews of European or American origin but also a lower quality of education. Jews of North African–Middle Eastern origin are progressively less represented in secondary and post-secondary education (the quantitative dimension) and in addition (in the qualitative dimension) perform less well on standardized tests, predominate in "second-rate, non-academic schools," have "inferior accomplishments" in higher education and are "under-represented in the high status fields of study—i.e., engineering, natural and mathematical sciences, and especially medicine."[102] It is a common pattern around the world—and a pattern commonly ignored by those who automatically attribute all intergroup income differences between individuals with the "same" education (quantitatively defined) to employer discrimination. In the employment market, both blacks and untouchables at the higher levels have advanced substantially while those at the lower levels show no such advancement and even some signs of retrogression. These patterns are also broadly consistent with patterns found in countries in which majorities have created preferences for themselves, in an effort to overtake more educationally or economically advanced minorities. These countries are also highly disparate among themselves.

These international patterns suggest that it is not the unique characteristics of each society or group but the incentives and mechanisms of preferential policies which explain the outcomes. Why these outcomes so often differ from the goals or rationales of preferential policies is a puzzle to be analyzed in the chapters that follow.

PART II

THE ILLUSIONS OF PREFERENTIAL POLICIES

CHAPTER FIVE

THE ILLUSION OF CONTROL AND KNOWLEDGE

In countries around the world, the empirical consequences of preferential policies have received much less attention than the rationales and goals of such policies. Too often these rationales and goals have been sufficient unto themselves, both in the political arena and in courts of law. Without even an attempt at empirical assessment of costs vs. benefits, with no attempt to pinpoint either losers or gainers, discussions of preferential policies are often exercises in assertion, counter-assertion, and accusation. Illusions flourish in such an atmosphere. So do the disappointments and bitterness to which illusions lead.

Several general kinds of illusions require special attention. First, there is the illusion of far more control of complex social interactions than anyone or any institution has been capable of exercising. In part this reflects an illusion of far more knowledge than anyone possesses. There has also been an illusion of morality where there has in fact been only a thin veneer of emotional rhetoric, seldom examined but often reiterated. In some countries there is yet another illusion—the illusion that preferential policies are compensating for wrongs suffered. These four illusions will be examined in this chapter and in the chapter that follows.

THE ILLUSION OF CONTROL

Temporal Control

Britain's Lord Scarman expressed a widespread view when he said:

> We can and for the present must accept the loading of the law in favour of one group at the expense of others, defending it as a temporary expedient in the balancing process which has to be undertaken when and where there is social and economic inequality.[1]

Similar views were expressed halfway around the world in India, where an advocate of preferential policies said: "Even the staunchest supporters of reservation acceded that it is a transitory provision."[2]

Widespread support of "temporary" preferences[3] is perhaps the clearest and simplest example of an illusion of control that has been subsequently mocked by the actual course of events. Neither majority nor minority preference policy has been temporary in practice, whether in Asia, Africa, North America, or Australia. Such policies have not only persisted but expanded as well, covering new benefits, new sectors, and in some countries, new groups. Even explicit cut-off dates in India and Pakistan did not stop this process, nor visibly slow it down. Yet the word "temporary" continues to be used in discussions of preferential policies—judicial and scholarly, as well as popular and political. No argument seems to be considered necessary to show that this transience can be enforced, so that the word "temporary" will be something more than political decoration. Indeed, few seem to feel a need to specify whether the dimensions of "temporary" are to be measured in actual units of time or by the attainment of some preconceived social results. If the latter, then the distinction between "temporary" and "eternal" can be wholly illusory in practice. In short, the nebulousness of the concept of "temporary" preference has matched its futility.

It is not only the temporal scope of preferential policies that has gotten beyond the control of its advocates. The spread of preferences to other groups—often groups successively further removed from the original rationale of the policy—represents just one of the other dimensions to escape control. These two things can of course happen simultaneously. The ability of preferential policies to go far beyond both their assigned limits of time and their initial rationales is perhaps most dramatically illustrated in Pakistan.

According to a study of Pakistani preferences, "the most potent original rationale for the quota system" was to ameliorate socioeconomic differences between East Pakistan and West Pakistan.[4] The desperately poor Bengalis of East Pakistan were "under-represented" in the civil service, the military, business, and the professions.[5] Even the administration of East Pakistan was filled with West Pakistanis.[6] Preferential policies to correct this were advocated in 1949 as "temporary" expedients to be phased out in 5 to 10 years.[7] In reality, however, these policies have lasted decades beyond this time and in 1984 were extended to 1994 by the late President Zia.[8] Not only did preferential quotas spread well beyond people from the East Pakistan region; they persist and are extensive and ever more complex today—long after East Pakistan broke away in 1971 to form the independent nation of Bangladesh. In short, those who provided the initial rationale for preferential policies have now disappeared by secession but the policies themselves are more extensive than ever.

In the United States, centuries of slavery and oppression of blacks provided the initial rationale for preferential policies which have been extended successively to groups which today add up to about two-thirds of the entire American population.[9] Each step in the extension may have seemed a small one, but the whole extension covers a vast spectrum. Obviously, if historic wrongs were to be righted, the indigenous American Indians also had important moral claims to preferences. Then too, bitter injustices against immigrants from China and Japan were also part of the national history, so Asians were added to the list. Once this happened, a businessman from India, entering the United States in the late twentieth century, was legally entitled to preferential benefits as an Asian,[10] even though people from India have higher incomes in the United States than the incomes of white Americans. From slaves toiling in the cotton fields under the lash to an affluent Indian owner of his own computer company in Silicon Valley is a long distance. However, that distance was not covered in one jump but by incremental extensions of the preferential principle over the years.

In India, as well, a very similar process has extended preferential benefits from poverty-stricken untouchables to prosperous members of politically dominant local majorities in a number of states. These locally dominant majority recipients of benefits for "other backward classes" now outnumber the untouchables. In short, neither the duration nor the scope of preferential policies has proved to be controllable in practice, however often it has been assumed to be in countries around the world.

Incentives and Attitudes

Behind the failure to control either the duration or the scope of preferential policies is a more fundamental and broader failure to see these policies as setting up *incentives* as well as goals. These incentives acquire a life of their own, independent of—and often counter to—the avowed goals of preferential policies. Nor are these simply isolated "mistakes" that can be "corrected." They are the fruition of fundamental misconceptions of the degree of control that can be maintained over a whole galaxy of complex social interactions.

At the individual level, the potential beneficiary and the potential loser are not mere blocks of wood passively placed where the policy dictates. Nor are they automatons who continue acting as before, except for modifications specified for them by others. Rather, they respond *in their own ways* to preferential policies. One of these ways was exemplified by the question asked in India's city of Hyderabad: "Are we not entitled to jobs just because we are not as qualified?" A Nigerian likewise wrote of "the tyranny of skills."[11] The sense of entitlement—independent of skills or performance—has long been an accompaniment of preferential policies, for the most disparate groups in the most disparate societies.

The late South African economist W. H. Hutt pointed out long ago that the most "virulent" white supporters of early racial preferential policies in the mines were "those who had not troubled to qualify themselves for promotion,"[12] and who therefore relied on being white instead. Today, in the Virgin Islands, even school children excuse their own substandard academic and behavioral performance by pointing out that government jobs will be waiting for them, as U.S. citizens[13]—jobs for which their better-behaved and better-performing West Indian classmates are ineligible. In Malaysia, likewise, "Malay students, who sense that their future is assured, feel less pressure to perform."[14] A study of black colleges in the United States similarly noted that even students planning post-graduate study often showed no sense of urgency about needing to be prepared "because they believe that certain rules would simply be set aside for them."[15] In India, even a fervent advocate of the untouchables, and of preferential policies for them, has urged untouchable students in medical and engineering schools to abandon their "indifference."[16]

The disincentives created by group preferences apply to both preferred and non-preferred groups. As W. H. Hutt wrote of the South African "color bar," these racial preferences "have vitiated the efficiency of the non-Whites by destroying incentives" and have also "weakened incentives to efficiency on the part of the Whites who have been feather-bedded."[17] A very similar principle is found in the very different setting of Jamaica, after it became independent and black-run. There it was the whites who faced the disincentives of the non-preferred. Many withdrew from the competition for public office because they "felt that the day of the black man had come and questioned why they had to make the effort if the coveted job or the national honor would go to the blacks, despite their qualifications."[18] In short, preferential policies represent not simply a transfer of benefits from one group to another, but can also represent a net loss, as both groups perform less well as a result.

Those who initiate preferential policies cannot sufficiently control the reactions of either preferred or non-preferred groups to ensure that such policies will have the desired effect, or even more in the desired direction. Counterproductive reactions that reduce national prosperity or social tranquility adversely affect even members of the preferred group, who are also members of the general society. Whether their gains in one role exceed their losses in the other role is an empirical question whose answer depends on the specifics of each situation. One of the clearly undesired and uncontrolled consequences of preferential policies has been a backlash by non-preferred groups. This backlash has ranged from campus racial incidents in the United States[19] to a bloody civil war in Sri Lanka.[20]

Honors

Nowhere is control more illusory than in the awarding of honors, whose very meaning and effect depend upon other people's opinions. Preferential honors for members of particular groups can easily render suspect not only those particular honors but also honors fully merited and awarded after free and open competition. If one-fifth the honors received by preferred groups are awarded under double standards, the other four-fifths are almost certain to fall under a cloud of suspicion as well, if only because some of those who lost out in the competition would prefer to believe that they were not bested fairly. It is by no means clear that more real honors—which are ultimately other people's opinions—will come to a group preferentially given awards. Preferential honors can in practice mean a moratorium on recognition of the group's achievements, which can be confounded with patronage or pay-offs. This need not inevitably be so. The point is that the matter is out of the control of those who decide award policy, and in the hands of others observing the outcomes and deciding what to make of them.

Honor is more than a sop to personal vanity. It is a powerful incentive which accomplishes many social tasks, including tasks that are too arduous and dangerous to be compensated by money—even inducing individuals in crisis situations to sacrifice their lives for the greater good of others. In more mundane matters, honor and respect from ones colleagues and subordinates are important and sometimes indispensable aids to cooperation, without which even the most talented and conscientious individuals sometimes cannot fulfill their promise. To jeopardize the respect and recognition of individuals from preferred groups by awarding "honors" tainted with double standards is not only to downgrade their own achievements but also to downgrade their chances of accomplishing those achievements in the first place.

Minority faculty members have often complained about a lack of intellectual and research interaction with their colleagues, and of being thought of as "affirmative action" professors.[22] After the media revealed that black students were admitted to the Harvard Medical School with lower qualifications, white patients began to refuse to be examined by such students.[23] The negative effects of tainted honors are by no means limited to academia.

Partial Preferences

The illusion of control includes the belief that preferential policies can be extended *part-way* into a process while maintaining equal treatment in the remainder of the process. For example, in the early days of "affirmative action" in the United States, it was sometimes asserted that special efforts to recruit minority employees or minority students would be followed by equal treatment at the actual selection stage and afterwards. Special concern for particular groups might also mean only special scrutiny to see that they were treated equally. President John F. Kennedy's Executive Order No. 10,925 required that employers who were government contractors "take affirmative action to ensure that the applicants are employed, and that employees are treated during employment without regard to race, creed, color, or national origin." That is virtually the antithesis of what affirmative action has come to mean today, either in the United States or in other countries where the term refers to statistical results viewed precisely *with regard* to race, color, creed, or national origin.

The concept of preferential concern, stopping part-way into a process, is not confined to employment or to the United States. In India, for example, a government minister has urged a small lowering of university admissions standards for students from scheduled castes and tribes, with the proviso that "he was recommending relaxation for admission and not for passing or grading."[24] Similar views were once expressed in the United States, where special recruitment programs for minority students quickly led to lower admissions standards for them—and this in turn led to "affirmative grading," to prevent excessive failures by minority students.[25] Double standards in grading may originate with the individual professor or be a result of administrative efforts or pressures.[26] Halfway around the world—in Soviet Central Asia—professors are also pressured to give preferential grading to Central Asian students.[27] In Malaysia, preferential grading is virtually institutionalized:

> Although grading is supposed to be without reference to ethnicity, all grades must be submitted to an evaluation review committee having heavy Malay representation. Individual faculty members report various instances when grades were unilaterally raised, apparently for purposes of "ethnic balance."[28]

Sometimes preferential grading takes the less direct form of creating special or easier subjects for particular groups, such as Maori Studies in New Zealand, Malay Studies in Singapore, or a variety of ethnic studies in the United States.

Whether in employment, education, or other areas, carefully limited or fine-tuned preferences have repeatedly proved to be illusory. Neither time limitations nor other limitations have in fact stopped their persistence and spread.

THE ILLUSION OF KNOWLEDGE

Among the reasons why control of the consequences of preferential policies has so often proven to be illusory is that effective control would require far more knowledge than anyone possesses or can realistically expect to possess. Much of what has been thought to be knowledge in this area is reiterated assumption, unchecked against any facts, though often dressed in the garb of statistical formulae, having the appearance of scientific objectivity. These underlying assumptions must be examined and tested against evidence—which often points in the opposite direction—and some of the statistical concepts must also be scrutinized and their implications and limitations clarified.

The Randomness Assumption

Preferential policies in some countries are predicated on a prior determination of discrimination against those now chosen as recipients of compensatory preferences. Statistical disparities between groups are often the sole evidence cited as proof of discrimination. Implicit in this approach is the assumption that disparities in excess of those attributable to random chance can be regarded as *prima facie* evidence of adverse actions by individuals, institutions, or "society" against the group for whom compensatory preferences are sought. If the statistical disparities are not regarded as conclusive evidence, they at least shift the burden of proof to those accused of discrimination. The growing familiarity of this procedure does not establish its logical or empirical validity. Its underlying reasoning is not essentially different from that of the familiar polemical device of claiming "it is no accident" that this or that episode occurred—the whole spectrum of possibilities being arbitrarily narrowed to (1) accident or (2) the particular explanation being promoted.

Some U.S. Supreme Court Justices have taken this approach to its logical extreme. Where white applicants have outperformed black applicants, the differential has been attributed to prior societal discrimination and the court's task has then been defined as restoring the particular individuals involved to where they would have been, but for the offending discrimination.[29] All this presupposes a range of knowledge that no one has ever possessed.

What would the average Englishman be like today "but for" the Norman conquest? What would the average Japanese be like "but for" the enforced isolation of Japan for two and a half centuries under the Tokugawa shoguns? What would the Middle East be like "but for" the emergence of Islam? In any other context besides preferential policy issues, the presumption of knowing the answers to such questions would be regarded as ridiculous, even as intellectual speculation, much less as a basis for concrete governmental action.

To know how one group's employment, education, or other pattern differs statistically from another's is usually easy. What is difficult to know are the many variables determining the interest, skill, and performance of those individuals from various groups who are being considered for particular jobs, roles, or institutions. What is virtually impossible to know are the patterns that would exist in a non-discriminatory world—the deviations from which would indicate the existence and magnitude of discrimination.

Age distribution and geographic distribution are only two very simple factors which can play havoc with the assumption that groups would be evenly or randomly distributed in occupations and institutions, in the absence of discrimination. When one group's median age is a decade younger than another's—not at all uncommon—that alone may be enough to cause the younger group to be statistically "over-represented" in sports, crime, and entry-level jobs, as well as in those kinds of diseases and accidents that are more prevalent among the young, while the older group is over-represented in homes for the elderly, in the kinds of jobs requiring long years of experience, and in the kinds of diseases and accidents especially prevalent among older people.

Another very simple factor operating against an even "representation" of groups is that many ethnic groups are distributed geographically in patterns differing from one another.[30] It would be unlikely that American ethnic groups concentrated in cold states like Minnesota and Wisconsin would be as well represented among citrus growers and tennis players as they are on hockey teams and among skiers. It is also unlikely that groups concentrated in landlocked states would be equally represented in maritime activities, or that groups from regions lacking mineral deposits would be as well represented among miners or in other occupations associated with extractive industries as groups located in Pennsylvania or West Virginia.

Differences in geographic concentrations among racial and ethnic groups are by no means confined to the U.S. In Brazil, people of German and Japanese ancestry are concentrated in the south. In Switzerland, whole regions are predominantly French, German, or Italian. In countries around the world, an overwhelming majority of the Chinese or the Jewish population are heavily concentrated in a few major cities[31]—often in just one city in a given country. Group differences in geographical distribution can reach right down to the neighborhood level or even to particular streets. In Buenos Aires, people of Italian ancestry have concentrated in particular neighborhoods or on particular streets, according to the places of their own or their ancestral origins in Italy.[32] In Bombay, people from different parts of India are likewise concentrated in particular neighborhoods or on particular streets.[33]

Lest the point be misunderstood,[34] while these two simple and obvious factors—age and location—are capable of disrupting the even "representation" that many assume to exist in the absence of discrimination, there are also innumerable other factors, of varying degrees of complexity and influence, that can do the same. Moreover, differences in age and location may play a significant role in explaining *some* socioeconomic differences between *some* groups but not other socioeconomic differences between those groups, or among other groups. The purpose here is not to pinpoint the reasons for intergroup differences—or even to assume that they can all be pinpointed—but rather to show how arbitrary and unfounded is the assumption that groups would be evenly "represented," in the absence of discrimination. Precisely because the known differences among groups are large and multi-dimensional, the presumption of weighing these differences so comprehensively and accurately as to know where some group would be "but for" discrimination approaches hubris.

Even the more modest goal of knowing the *general direction* of the deviation of a group's position from where it would have been without discrimination is by no means necessarily achievable. What are the "effects" of centuries of injustice, punctuated by recurring outbursts of lethal mass violence, against the overseas Chinese in Southeast Asia or against the Jews in Europe? Both groups are generally more prosperous than their persecutors. Would they have been still more prosperous in the absence of such adversity? Perhaps—but many peoples with a long history of peace, and with prosperity supplied by nature itself, have quietly stagnated. This is not to say that the Jews and the Chinese would have done so. It is only to say that *we do not know and cannot know.* No amount of good intentions will make us omniscient. No fervent invocation of "social justice" will supply the missing knowledge.

The idea that large statistical disparities between groups are unusual—and therefore suspicious—is commonplace, but only among those who have not bothered to study the history of racial, ethnic, and other groups in countries around the world. Among leading scholars who have in fact devoted years of research to such matters, a radically different picture emerges. Professor Donald L. Horowitz of Duke University, at the end of a massive and masterful international study of ethnic groups—a study highly praised in scholarly journals[35]—examined the idea of a society where groups are "proportionately represented" at different levels and in different sectors. He concluded, "few, if any, societies have ever approximated this description."[36]

A world-wide study of military forces and police forces by Professor Cynthia Enloe of Clark University likewise concluded that "militaries fall far short of mirroring, even roughly, the multi-ethnic societies" from which they come.[37] Moreover, just "as one is unlikely to find a police force or a military that mirrors its plural society, so one is unlikely to find a representative bureaucracy."[38] One reason is that "it is common for different groups to rely on different mobility ladders."[39] Some choose the military, some the bureaucracy, and some various parts of the private sector. Even within the military, different branches tend to have very different racial or ethnic compositions[40]—the Afrikaners, for example, being slightly under-represented in the South African navy and greatly over-represented in the South African army,[41] though their utter dominance in the government ensures that they cannot be discriminated against in either branch. Powerless minorities have likewise been greatly over-represented or even dominant in particular branches of the military or the police—the Chinese in Malaysia's air force and among detectives in the police force, for example.[42]

In the private sector as well, it is commonplace for minorities to be over-represented, or even dominant, in competitive industries where they have no power to prevent others from establishing rival businesses. Jewish prominence in the clothing industry, not only in the United States, but in Argentina and Chile as well,[43] did not reflect any ability to prevent other Americans or Argentines from manufacturing garments, but simply the advantages of the Jews' having brought needle-trade skills and experience with them from Eastern Europe.[44] The fact that Jews owned more than half the clothing stores in mid-nineteenth-century Melbourne[45] likewise reflected that same advantage, rather than any ability to forbid other Australians from selling clothes. In a similar way, German minorities have been dominant as pioneers in piano manufacturing in colonial America, Czarist Russia, Australia, France, and England.[46] Italian fishermen, Japanese farmers, and Irish politicians have been among many other minority groups with special success in special fields, without any ability to keep out others.

Another distinguished scholar who has studied multiethnic societies around the world, M.I.T. Professor Myron Weiner, refers to "the universality of ethnic inequality." He points out that those inequalities are multi-dimensional:

> All multi-ethnic societies exhibit a tendency for ethnic groups to engage in different occupations, have different levels (and, often, types) of education, receive different incomes, and occupy a different place in the social hierarchy.[47]

Yet the pattern Professor Weiner has seen, after years of research, as a "universality" is routinely assumed to be an *anomaly,* not only by preferential policy advocates, but also by the intelligentsia, the media, legislators, and judges—all of whom tend to assume, as a *norm,* what Professor Horowitz has found to exist (or even to be approximated) in "few, if any, societies." That what exists widely across the planet is regarded as an anomaly, while what exists virtually nowhere is regarded as a norm, is a tribute to the effectiveness of sheer reiteration in establishing a vision—and of the difficulties of dispelling a prevailing vision by facts.

Some might try to salvage the statistical argument for discrimination by describing discrimination as also being universal. However, groups who are in no position to discriminate against anybody have often been over-represented in coveted positions—the Chinese in Malaysian universities, the Tamils in Sri Lankan universities, the southerners in Nigerian universities, and Asians in American universities being just some of the minorities of whom this is true. All sorts of other powerless minorities have dominated particular industries or sectors of the economy, the intellectual community, or government employment. Large statistical disparities are commonplace, both in the presence of discrimination and in its absence. Indeed, large disparities have been commonplace in the utilization of preferential programs designed to reduce disparities.

The intellectual and political *coup* of those who promote the randomness assumption is to put the burden of proof entirely on others. It is not merely the individual employer, for example, who must disprove this assumption in his own particular case, in order to escape a charge of discrimination. All who oppose the randomness assumption find themselves confronted with the task of disproving an elusive plausibility, for which no evidence is offered. As for counterevidence, no enumeration of the myriad ways in which groups are grossly disparate—in age of marriage,[48] alcohol consumption,[49] immigration patterns,[50] performance in sports,[51] performance on tests[52]—can ever be conclusive, even when extended past the point where the patience of the audience is exhausted.

Those viscerally convinced of the pervasiveness of discrimination and its potency as an explanation of social disparities—and convinced also of the effectiveness of preferential policies as a remedy—are little troubled by the logical shakiness of the statistical evidence. That is all the more reason for others to be doubly troubled—not simply because an incorrect policy may be followed but also, and more importantly, because actions ostensibly based on the rule of law are in substance based on visceral convictions, the essence of lynch law.

Statistical "Control" and "Explanation"

Those who regard income differences or occupational differences between groups as evidences of discrimination recognize that groups also differ in education, job experience, and other factors that affect such results as incomes and occupations. However, by comparing individuals with the same education, the same job experience, etc., who belong to different racial or ethnic groups, they treat the remaining differentials in pay or occupational status as evidence of discrimination and as a rough measure of its magnitude. In principle, this process of statistically controlling variables that affect outcomes is logical and reasonable. It is only in practice that serious problems arise because we simply do not know enough to do what we are trying to do or claiming to do.

A 1982 study by the U.S. Commission on Civil Rights, for example, recognized that differences in age and education affect incomes but considered that its study of intergroup economic differences was "controlling for such factors"[53] when it compared individuals of the same age and with the same number of years of schooling. Unfortunately, education is one of many *multi-dimensional* variables. Education varies not only in number of years, but also qualitatively, according to the calibre of the institution in which the education was received, the performance of the student receiving the education, and the kind of field in which the student specialized. Seldom are statistical data sufficiently detailed to permit holding all these dimensions of education constant. Moreover, qualitative variables such as the calibre of the institution are difficult to quantify and impossible to quantify with precision.

One way of dealing with this complication is to ignore the multi-dimensional nature of education, either by explicitly or implicitly assuming that these individual variations more or less cancel out when comparing thousands of people. However, individuals from different racial or ethnic groups differ not only randomly but also systematically. For example, groups with significantly lower quantities of education tend to have lower qualities of education as well, whether quality is measured by individual performance, institutional ranking, or the prestige and remuneration of the fields of specialization. This pattern is found, whether comparing Chinese versus Malays in Malaysia, Tamils versus Sinhalese in Sri Lanka, European and American Jews versus North African and Middle Eastern Jews in Israel, caste Hindus versus untouchables in India, or whites versus blacks or Hispanics in the United States.[54] In short, what is called the "same" education in intergroup statistical comparisons is often not even approximately the same education in reality.

The difference that these multiple dimensions can make may be illustrated by one of the few studies that attempted to control the qualitative dimensions of education—a study comparing the salaries of faculty members from different racial backgrounds. Among its variables were (1) possession or non-possession of a Ph.D.; (2) the professional ranking of the department from which the Ph.D. was obtained; (3) the field of specialization; and (4) the number of articles published by the faculty member. In gross terms—that is, controlling for none of these variables—white faculty had a higher average salary than black faculty. But when blacks and whites in the same field were compared, blacks had higher salaries than whites in the social sciences and the natural sciences, while whites had higher salaries in the humanities. When comparing blacks and whites who both had Ph.D.s from highly rated departments, blacks earned more than whites in all three areas. Among faculty members with Ph.D.s from lower-ranked departments, however, whites still had higher salaries than blacks. Blacks with Ph.D.s earned higher salaries in the social sciences and whites with Ph.D.s earned more in the natural sciences. Among faculty members with Ph.D.s and 5 or more articles published, blacks had higher salaries than whites in all three fields, when both had their doctorates from the same quality level of institution.[55]

In short, the very same raw data can tell not only a different story, but even an opposite story, according to how much they are disaggregated or how many variables are held constant. Ultimately the researcher is limited by the available data and the dimensions it covers. These particular data happened to cover qualitative dimensions that are often lacking. This good fortune resulted from the long-standing practice of academic professions to rank graduate departments in their own respective fields. What is more generally relevant to the use of statistics in preferential policy analysis is that individuals with apparently the "same" education along one dimension may have very different education along other dimensions. Put differently, groups are not distributed randomly or the same among the various dimensions. In this particular example, black faculty had a Ph.D. less than half as frequently as white faculty, the Ph.D.s received by black faculty were from high-quality institutions less than half as often, and were concentrated in fields with lower average earnings. Finally, black faculty published far less than white faculty.[56]

These data also happened to include Asian faculty members. Their distribution in all these respects differed substantially from the distributions of either blacks or whites.[57] Such multi-dimensional differences among groups are commonplace around the world, however often random or proportionate distribution is *assumed* in discussions of preferential policy. In India, for example, an attempt to compare untouchable medical school students and caste Hindu medical school students of the same social characteristics proved futile when individuals from the two groups who were similar in specified characteristics turned out, during lengthy interviews, to be very dissimilar in characteristics not specified at the outset but clearly relevant to their medical education.

Beginning with untouchable and caste Hindu "students matched individually" by "some important background characteristics" such as father's occupation, income, or language,[58] Indian scholar P. R. Velaskar later discovered that "the match group is not perfectly matched as originally planned"[59]—a considerable under-statement, for the illiteracy rate among the fathers and grandfathers of the untouchable medical school students was several times as high as among the other medical school students' fathers and grandfathers.[60] Understandably, the untouchable students had had parental guidance in their education less often than the other students had,[61] the homes from which they came contained far fewer books[62] and their pre-college schools were not as good.[63] They were not meaningfully the same, even though the same on the particular socioeconomic characteristics initially specified.

Multi-dimensional differences are not statistically "controlled" by holding one dimension constant, even when that is the only dimension on which data are available. Moreover, not all differences are quantifiable, nor all non-quantifiable differences negligible in their effect on outcomes. Where statistics are able to capture only some of the relevant dimensions—to "control" only some of the variables—the assumption that remaining disparities represent discrimination is implicitly an assumption that groups are distributed similarly in the unexamined dimensions, however disparately they are distributed in the variables for which we have data.

Just as statistical "control" for variables that differ among groups often fails to control, so statistical "explanations" often fail to explain in any but the most narrow definitional sense used by statisticians. When two groups differ in some way—in income, for example—and 20 percent of that difference is eliminated by holding constant some factor x (years of education, for example), then *in a purely definitional sense,* statisticians say that factor x "explains" 20 percent of the difference between the groups. Unfortunately, as arguments develop, their initial special definitions and assumptions tend to fade into the background, with the statistical results becoming correspondingly inflated as to their scope and validity.

The potential for misleading explanations can be illustrated with a simple example. Shoe size undoubtedly correlates with test scores on advanced mathematics examinations, in the sense that people with size 3 shoes probably cannot, on average, answer as many questions correctly as people with size 12 shoes—the former being much more likely to be younger children and the latter more likely to be older children or adults. Thus shoe size "explains" part of the math score difference—in the special sense in which statisticians use the word. But nobody can expect to do better on a math test by wearing larger shoes on the day it is taken. In the real sense of the word, shoe size *explains* nothing.

When a statistician testifies in court that his data can "explain" only 40 percent of income disparities between groups by "controlling" for age, education, urbanization, and whatever other variable may be cited, the judge and jury may not realize how little the words "explain" and "control" mean in this context. Judge and jury may conclude that the other 60 percent must represent discrimination. But virtually no statistical study can control for all the relevant variables simultaneously, because the in-depth data, especially along qualitative dimensions, are often simply not available. By controlling for the available variables and implicitly assuming that the unaccounted-for variables do not differ significantly between groups, one can generate considerable residual "unexplained" statistical disparity and equate that with discrimination—or with genes, if one's thinking runs in that direction.

Looked at another way, groups with visible, quantifiable disadvantages often have other, not-so-visible, not-so-quantifiable disadvantages as well. If statistics manage to capture the effects of the first kinds of disadvantages, the effects of the second kind become part of an unexplained residual. It is arbitrary to call that residual "discrimination." Merely substituting genes for discrimination would, by the same reasoning and with the same statistical data, lead to the radically different conclusion that racial "superiority" or "inferiority" determined outcomes. Both conclusions depend on arbitrarily making some selected factor—whether discrimination or genes or something else—the residual beneficiary of our inability to account comprehensively for the variations widely found in the real world, whether between groups or within groups.

Statistical Trends

Assessing the actual net effect of a policy on any group requires more than simple before-and-after comparisons. Yet much discussion of the effects of preferential policies proceed as if there were a stationary situation, to which "change" was added. In the United States, for example, it is an often-cited fact that the proportion of blacks in professional and other high-level occupations rose substantially in the years following passage of the Civil Rights Act of 1964. It is an almost totally ignored fact that the proportion of blacks in such occupations rose even more substantially in the years *preceding* passage of the Civil Rights Act of 1964.[64] It is an equally ignored fact that the incomes of Asian Americans and Mexican Americans rose substantially—both absolutely and relative to that of the general population—in the years preceding passage of the Civil Rights Act of 1964 and its evolution into preferential policies.[65]

Similar patterns appear in other countries, where it was precisely the rise of a newly educated and upwardly mobile class that led to demands for preferential policies. In Bombay, for example, the "marked advancement of the Maharashtrians occurred prior to the stringent policy measures adopted by the state government" to promote preferential hiring.[66] In part this reflected a prior "enormous growth in school enrollments in Maharashtra" and a "rapid expansion in college enrollment"—also prior to preferences.[67] A similar growth of an indigenous, newly educated class in Poland, Czechoslovakia, and Lithuania during the years between the two World Wars led to demands for preferential policies in the form of group quotas to relieve them from having to compete with Jews.[68] Likewise, in Nigeria, it was the recent growth of an educated class in the north that led to demands for preferential policies to relieve them from having to compete with southern Nigerians.[69] This same pattern of a rising educated class prior to the preferential policies that they promote can also be found in Indonesia, Sri Lanka, Malaysia, the Quebec province of Canada, and much of sub-Saharan Africa.[70]

Any assessment of preferential policies must take account of pre-existing trends, rather than assume a static world to which "change" is added. It must also avoid generalizing from trends in particular sectors to national trends. Even in countries where nationwide data on the economic position of officially preferred groups show little or no improvement, nevertheless improvements in particular sectors may be dramatic. Comparisons between sectors of the economy that are more closely tied to government and those that are more independently part of the private sector have consistently shown the rise of officially preferred groups to be greater in the government and government-related sectors—whether in India, Poland, Malaysia, Hungary, Sri Lanka, or the United States.[71] Some advocates of such policies consider this to be decisive evidence of their effectiveness. But nationwide statistics for the very same groups over the very same spans of time often contradict this.

How is this possible? In an economy with a substantial private sector, the special demand for particular groups in government-related employment may result in considerable *transfer* of that group's employment—which is then seen as a dramatic *increase* in the areas to which they transfer and their rise to important positions there as symptomatic of a general rise in the economy as a whole. But this ignores the possibility of a corresponding decrease in other sectors. In the United States, for example, the employment of blacks by private employers without government contracts *declined* between 1970 and 1980,[72] while increases in black employment in various government and government-related sectors were being hailed as indicators of the general progress of blacks under affirmative action.

Conversely, a decline in the quantity and quality of government-related employment does not mean an overall decline. In the United States, during the period from the beginning of the Woodrow Wilson administration to the beginning of the Franklin D. Roosevelt administration, the position of blacks in the federal civil service declined dramatically. The number of black postmasters was approximately cut in half and blacks were forced out of the military, and especially naval, forces as well.[73] Yet the occupational position of blacks nationally did not retrogress, and in fact advanced slightly.[74] We cannot generalize from what happens in government or government-related employment, or in any particular firm or sector of the economy.

CHAPTER SIX

THE ILLUSION OF MORALITY AND COMPENSATION

Virtually all preferential policies have a moral rationale. Even preferences for majorities are seldom content to rest explicitly on brute power and narrow self-interest, but reflect a need for some moral patina, often felt to be genuine. In recent times, as social concerns have shifted toward the plight of less fortunate minorities, moral justifications have often been in terms of *compensatory* policies, designed to offset disadvantages which handicap their efforts at advancement. Compensatory policies can also be directed at majorities, as in Malaysia or Sri Lanka, for example.

General questions of morality will be examined first and then the complex question of compensatory preferences will be considered separately.

THE ILLUSION OF MORALITY

A wide variety of moral arguments has been used to justify preferential policies for majorities and minorities. Some of these arguments have little in common, except for being largely unexamined in the excitement of crusading zeal—and being successful politically. Among the reasons given for preferences are that (1) the group is innately superior; (2) the group is indigenous; (3) the group has been historically wronged; and (4) the group happens to be less well represented in desirable institutions or occupations, for whatever reason, so that this "imbalance" must be "corrected."

Innate Superiority

So much time, emotion, and energy have gone into refuting claims of innate superiority that relatively few have paused to reflect that accepting the claim of superiority, for the sake of argument, might make the assertion of entitlement even more ridiculous. Anyone who claimed to be a superior runner and demanded that he therefore be allowed to start the race 10 yards ahead of his inferior competitors would be unlikely to convince anyone. Yet, historically, the argument that superiority deserves official preference has carried the day politically in such disparate settings as the "Jim Crow" South, Nazi Germany, South Africa, and in many colonial regimes. In such cases, however, the argument has not had to convince others logically or empirically, but only to evoke a sense of solidarity within a group already possessed of the political power needed to give themselves special benefits.

This special case has more general implications, however. The explicit arguments for preferences are not necessarily the *reasons* for preferences, particularly among the beneficiaries. Neither logic nor evidence is necessary politically, while emotional reiteration may be sufficient. Moreover, whatever the arguments for preferential policies, these preferences can long outlive the validity of those arguments, whether the degree of validity be zero or 100 percent, or anywhere in between. For example, a genuinely disadvantaged group can cling to preferences, or seek more, long after their disadvantages have been redressed. The moral question, therefore, is not simply whether particular groups deserve particular benefits for particular periods of time, or until particular social conditions are achieved. The real question is whether the *actual consequences of the particular processes* being initiated are likely to be justified, morally or otherwise.

Indigenousness

A more readily established claim is that of being indigenous. However, the logic that turns that fact into a moral claim is by no means obvious. Like claims of innate superiority, claims of being indigenous evoke a sense of solidarity within the beneficiary group. Unlike claims of superiority, however, claims of indigenousness often evoke feelings of moral support from outside the beneficiary group. The question is what basis there is for anyone who is not indigenous to take seriously such moral claims by those who are.

Where an indigenous group was once invaded, dispossessed of its lands, or otherwise mistreated by conquerors, the moral condemnation of the latter is based on their actions, not on the indigenousness of the victims. Had they done the same things to people who had settled within the prior century, that would not make it any more right or wrong. Moreover, claims of indigenous preference are not limited to such situations. Malays today claim privileges based on being "sons of the soil"—not against the British, who were the colonial power, but against the Chinese and the Indians, who were not. Similar preferential claims have been advanced by the indigenous peoples of Fiji, Burma, Uganda, and other countries, against groups who never conquered them or even tried to.

One reason why indigenous victims may seem especially wronged is that the toil of untold generations may have gone into producing what was taken from them. But, again, this may be equally true (or more true) of people who cannot claim to be indigenous. Were England to be invaded, conquered, and plundered, that would be widely condemned, even though no one familiar with their history would claim that the English are the indigenous people of England. Moreover, in many parts of the world, the indigenous peoples have built few material things of a lasting nature and the conquerors have built much, so that a reconquest by descendants of the original inhabitants would represent more plunder than the original conquest. So too would a governmental transfer of what has been created in the meantime.

One of the recurring themes in moral arguments for indigenous preferences is the linkage of the indigenous people to their native soil. Phrases like "sons of the soil," in various countries, evoke this image. However, human beings have not created land. Whether indigenous or not, their occupation of it as a group has largely been based on force. When one conquering people is in turn conquered by another, observers may deplore the bloodshed and plunder, but it is difficult to see what moral claim the losing side has against the winners, who have simply been more efficient or more lucky in pursuing the same goals as themselves. Here as elsewhere, where injustice has been done, it is the injustice that is morally significant, not the indigenousness of the victim.

Even in places and times where no credible claim of conquest or plunder can be made against a non-native, non-preferred group, there is often still a feeling that the indigenous people are entitled to preferential treatment in their own homeland. Little or no argument is usually offered for this assertion. At most there may be an allusion to the fact that most peoples "rule the roost" in their own homelands, and that there is psychic discomfort when "foreigners" (even many generations resident in the country) are unduly prominent in the economy or society. This is essentially an argument that what *is* in most places is what *ought* to be in all places. In addition to being a *non sequitur,* this assertion attributes to indigenousness a power that is usually due to being a numerical majority. At its worst, it is an argument that might makes right or an evocation of tribalism that need not be shared by observers who are not of that tribe, and which has no moral basis in any case.

Historical Compensation

The wrongs of history have been invoked by many groups in many countries as a moral claim for contemporary compensation. Much emotional fervor goes into such claims but the question here is about their logic or morality. Assuming for the sake of argument that the historical claims are factually correct, which may not be the case in all countries, to transfer benefits between two groups of living contemporaries because of what happened between two sets of dead people is to raise the question whether any sufferer is in fact being compensated. Only where both wrongs and compensation are viewed as collectivized and inheritable does redressing the wrongs of history have a moral, or even a logical, basis.

The biological continuity of the generations lends plausibility to the notion of group compensation—but only if guilt can be inherited. Otherwise there are simply windfall gains and windfall losses among contemporaries, according to the accident of their antecedents. Moreover, few people would accept this as a general principle to be applied consistently, however much they may advocate it out of compassion (or guilt) over the fate of particular unfortunates. No one would advocate that today's Jews are morally entitled to put today's Germans in concentration camps, in compensation for the Nazi Holocaust. Most people would not only be horrified at any such suggestion but would also regard it as a second act of gross immorality, in no way compensating the first, but simply adding to the sum total of human sins.

Sometimes a more sociological, rather than moral, claim is made that living contemporaries are suffering from the *effects* of past wrongs and that it is these effects which must be offset by compensatory preferences. Tempting as it is to imagine that the contemporary troubles of historically wronged groups are due to those wrongs, this is confusing causation with morality. The contemporary socioeconomic position of groups in a given society often bears no relationship to the historic wrongs they have suffered. Both in Canada and in the United States, the Japanese have significantly higher incomes than the whites, who have a documented history of severe anti-Japanese discrimination in both countries.[1] The same story could be told of the Chinese in Malaysia, Indonesia, and many other countries around the world, of the Jews in countries with virulent anti-Semitism, and a wide variety of other groups in a wide variety of other countries. Among poorer groups as well, the level of poverty often has little correlation with the degree of oppression. No one would claim that the historic wrongs suffered by Puerto Ricans in the United States exceed those suffered by blacks, but the average Puerto Rican income is lower than the average income of blacks.

None of this proves that historic wrongs have no contemporary effects. Rather, it is a statement about the limitations of our knowledge, which is grossly inadequate to the task undertaken and likely to remain so. To pretend to disentangle the innumerable sources of intergroup differences is an exercise in hubris rather than morality.

As one contemporary example of how easy it is to go astray in such efforts, it was repeated for years that the high rate of single-parent, teenage pregnancy among blacks was "a legacy of slavery." Evidence was neither asked nor given. But, when serious scholarly research was finally done on this subject, the evidence devastated this widely held belief. The vast majority of black children grew up in two-parent homes, even under slavery itself, and for generations thereafter.[2] The current levels of single-parent, teenage pregnancy are a phenomenon of the last half of the twentieth century and are a disaster that has also struck groups with wholly different histories from that of blacks.[3] Passionate commitment to "social justice" can never be a substitute for knowing what you are talking about.

Those who attribute any part of the socioeconomic fate of any group to factors internal to that group are often accused of "blaming the victim." This may sometimes be part of an attempt to salvage the historical compensation principle but it deserves separate treatment.

"Blame" and "Victims"

The illusion of morality is often confused with the reality of causation. If group A originates in a country where certain scientific and technological skills are widespread and group B originates in a country where they are not, then when they immigrate to the same third country, they are likely to be statistically "represented" to very different degrees in occupations and institutions requiring such skills. There is nothing mysterious about this, in causal terms. But those who wish to attribute this disparity to institutional discrimination are quick to respond to any mention of group B's lesser scientific-technological background as a case of "blaming the victim." By making the issue *who* is to blame, such arguments evade or pre-empt the more fundamental question—whether this is a matter of blame in the first place.

Clearly today's living generation—in any group—cannot be *blamed* for the centuries of cultural evolution that went on before they were born, often in lands that they have never seen. Nor can they be blamed for the fact that the accident of birth caused them to inherit one culture rather than another. In causal terms, it would be a staggering coincidence if cultures evolving in radically different historical circumstances were equally effective for all purposes when transplanted to a new society. Blame has nothing to do with it.

Grievance Versus "Justice"

Moralism confuses issues in many ways. For example, justifiable compassion for less fortunate people often shades off into an unjustifiable romanticizing of such people, their leaders, or their leaders' ideas and rhetoric. Groups seeking preferential treatment almost invariably say that they are seeking "justice," whether they are a majority or a minority, previously favored or disfavored, currently better off or worse off than others. When people want *more,* they call more "justice." But, when groups with a sense of grievance acquire power, whether locally or nationally, they seldom stop at redressing grievances and seldom exhibit impartial justice toward others.

Nothing is more common than for previously oppressed groups to oppress others when they get the chance. When Poles and Hungarians acquired their own independent nations after the First World War, they inaugurated a savage escalation of anti-Semitism. Similarly, after the Second World War, newly independent nations began oppressing their respective minorities from Indonesia to Sri Lanka to almost all of sub-Saharan Africa. This has included not only the usual forms of discrimination but also mob violence that has killed hundreds in Indonesia and Malaysia, thousands in Sri Lanka, and tens of thousands in Nigeria.

South Africa's white Afrikaners have long been a "grievance-fed" people, as South African economist W. H. Hutt called them.[4] Their leaders have kept alive for generations the grievances that caused them to launch a great trek away from British authority to settle new land in the nineteenth century, the grievances growing out of the two Boer wars they lost against the British, and the economic grievances they felt as a predominantly lower class in an economy dominated by British and Jewish businessmen and financiers. Some of these historic grievances were quite valid—for example, the 25,000 Afrikaner women and children who died in British concentration camps during the Second Boer War. However, as Hutt observed: "Races which grumble about the 'injustices' or 'oppressions' to which they are subjected can often be observed to be inflicting not dissimilar injustices upon other races."[5] The Afrikaners' escalation of anti-black laws when they first came to power in a coalition government in 1924 was only a foretaste of the evils of full-scale *apartheid* which they later imposed after they achieved unchallenged political dominance in 1948.

Similar patterns have existed in the United States. Just as the long-oppressed Irish became one of the groups most hostile to blacks, so today Koreans and Vietnamese refugees operating small businesses in black ghettoes in cities around the country are targets of racist propaganda and violence from local black leaders and those whom they incite. The arguments and demands made against them are the same as those made against the Jewish businessmen in the same ghettoes a generation earlier or against the Chinese businessmen in Southeast Asia, the Lebanese in Sierre Leone, or small retailing minority groups in countries around the world. What is different is that such racism on the part of some black leaders is passed over in silence by those who normally condemn racism, because their vision automatically casts blacks in the role of victims. But people do not cease being human beings just because they are labeled victims—and if the history of human beings shows anything, it shows repeatedly the desire for self-aggrandizement at the expense of others.

A sense of group grievance is seldom a prelude to just treatment of others. More often it hearlds a "Now it's our turn" attitude. No one felt or promoted a sense of being historically aggrieved more than Adolf Hitler.

"Under-Representation" and "Life Chances"

Quite aside from claims of historic wrongs, the argument has often been made—on grounds of morality as well as political or social expediency—that the "under-representation" of particular groups in desirable roles is an "imbalance" to be "corrected." Majorities have made such claims as readily as minorities, in circumstances where their only disadvantages were their own lack of skills or interest, as well as where a plausible case could be made that imposed disabilities have handicapped them.

Among the many unexamined assumptions behind preferential policies is the belief that intergroup friction is a function of the magnitude of their income gaps, so that more social harmony can be achieved by reducing these gaps. As with so much that has been said in this area, evidence has been neither asked nor given, while counter-evidence is plentiful, varied, and ignored.

In Bombay, the hostility of the Maharashtrians has been directed primarily at the South Indians, who are somewhat ahead of them economically, rather than against the Gujaratis, who are far ahead of them.[6] Throughout sub-Saharan Africa, there has historically been far more hostility directed by Africans against Asians than against Europeans, who are economically far ahead of both.[7] A similar pattern is found *within* African groups. In Nigeria, for example, the Yoruba were far ahead of the Ibo economically in 1940, while there was a much smaller gap at that time between the Hausa and the Ibo. Yet the hostility and violence between Hausa and Ibo in that era greatly exceeded any friction between either of these groups and the Yoruba. Later, as the Ibos rose, narrowing the gap between themselves and the Yoruba, it was precisely then that Ibo-Yoruba outbreaks of violence occurred.[8]

Advocates of preferential policies often express a related belief, similarly unsupported by evidence, that an even distribution of groups across sectors of the economy tends to reduce social frictions and hostility. Much history suggests the opposite, that "the ethnic division of labor is more a shield than a sword."[9]

The utter dominance of particular sectors by particular minority groups has been quietly accepted for generations in many countries—until a specific, organized campaign has been whipped up against the minority,[10] often by members of the majority who are seeking to enter the minority-dominated sector and are finding their competition very formidable. Often majority-group customers or suppliers actually prefer dealing with the minority-run entrepreneurs. "Indonesian peasants tended to prefer the Arabs,"[11] the Burmese preferred the Indians,[12] the Malays preferred dealing with the Chinese.[13] Even in the midst of ethnic riots against other groups, certain middleman minorities have been spared—the Greeks in the Sudan, Hindus in Burma, Marwaris in Assam.[14] Organized boycotts of minority businessmen have been spearheaded by majority-group business rivals, from Uganda and Kenya to the Philippines and the United States.[15] Contrary to what is widely (and lightly) assumed, neither an even representation of groups nor mass resentment at unevenness are "natural."

Repeatedly, in countries scattered around the world, it has been precisely the rise of newly emerging ethnic competitors—whether in business, government, or the professions—which has produced not only friction with groups already dominant in the sectors concerned but also, and much more importantly, has led the newcomers to whip up their whole group emotionally against the already established group. A Sri Lankan legislator noted this pattern early in that country's interethnic troubles:

> University graduates and people like that are the cause of all the trouble—not the vast mass of the Sinhalese people. It is those men, these middle-class unemployed seeking employment, who are jealous of the fact that a few Tamils occupy seats of office in Government—these are the people who have gone round the country-side, rousing the masses and creating this problem.[16]

Halfway around the world a similar charge was made, that "the educated Nigerian is the worst peddler of tribalism."[17] In the very different setting of Hungary in the 1880s, the promotion of anti-Semitism was largely the work of "students, country intellectuals and sections of the middle classes," while the Hungarian peasant masses remained relatively unresponsive.[18]

Advocates of preferential policies often see these policies as not only promoting social harmony by reducing gaps in income and "representation," but also as part of a more general attempt to "equalize life chances." Much effort is expended establishing the moral desirability of this goal and the extent to which we currently fall short of it, while little or no effort goes into establishing our *capability* to accomplish this staggering task. One clue to the magnitude and difficulty of what is being attempted are the various ways in which first-born children excel their siblings. A completely disproportionate number of the famous individuals in history were either first-born or the only child. In more mundane achievements as well, the first-born tend to excel. A study of National Merit Scholarship finalists showed that, even in five-child families, the first-born became finalists more often than all the other siblings combined. The same was true in two-, three-, and four-child families.[19] Such disparities, among people born of the same parents and raised under the same roof, mock presumptions of being able to equalize life chances across broader and deeper differences among people in a large, complex, and, especially, multi-ethnic society.

The abstract moral desirability of a goal cannot pre-empt the prior question of our capacity to achieve it. This is not even a question of falling short of all that might be hoped for. It is a question of risking counterproductive, disastrous, and even bloody results.

Beneficiaries and Losers

Part of the moral aura surrounding preferential policies is due to the belief that such policies benefit the less fortunate. The losers in this presumed redistribution are seldom specified, though the underlying assumption seems to be that they are the more fortunate.

Empirical evidence for such assumptions is largely lacking and the *a priori* case for believing them is unconvincing. For example, the effects of preferential policies depend on the costs of complementary factors required to use the preferences. These costs can obviously be borne more readily by those who are already more fortunate. Benefits set aside for businessmen of the preferred group are of no use to members of that group who do not happen to own a business, nor possess the capital to start one. Preferential admission to medical school is a benefit only to those who have already gone to college. Because preferential benefits tend to be concentrated on more lucrative or prestigious things, they are often within striking distance only for the fortunate few who have already advanced well beyond most other members of the preferred group. In Third World countries, where the great demand is for clerical jobs in the government, the poorer groups in these countries often have difficulty reaching even the modest level of education required for such employment.

In a number of countries, preferential policies—whether for a majority or a minority—have benefited, primarily or exclusively, the most fortunate segment of the groups designated as beneficiaries. In India's state of Tamil Nadu, for example, the highest of the so-called "backward classes" legally entitled to preferences, constituting 11 percent of the total "backward classes" population in that state, received almost half of all jobs and university admissions set aside for these classes, while lower castes—making up the bottom 12 percent of the "backward classes" population—received only 1 to 2 percent of the reserved jobs and university admissions.[20] In Malaysia, Malay students from families in the lower income brackets—63 percent of the population—received 14 percent of the university scholarships, while Malay students whose families were in the top 17 percent of the income distribution received just over half of all scholarships awarded to Malays.[21] In Sri Lanka, preferential university admissions for people from backward regions of the country appear likewise to have benefited primarily students from affluent families in these areas.[22]

Such results have sometimes been discussed as a maldistribution of benefits. But much more than that is involved. The less fortunate members of designated beneficiary groups have often not only failed to share proportionately in benefits but have actually retrogressed during the era of preferential policies. While the statistical representation of Malays on corporate boards of directors in Malaysia rose under preferential treatment policies,[23] so too did the proportion of Malays among the population living below the official poverty level.[24] In India, while the proportion of untouchables among high-level government officials has increased substantially during the era of preferential treatment,[25] so too has the proportion of untouchables who work as landless agricultural laborers.[26] In the United States, while blacks with college education or substantial job experience have advanced economically, both absolutely and relative to whites of the same description, during the era of preferential "goals and timetables," blacks with low levels of education and little job experience have fallen further behind whites of exactly the same description during the same span of time.[27] Those American minority businessmen who participate in the preferential program called business "set-asides" under Section 8(a) of the Small Business Act average a personal net worth of $160,000 each—not only far higher than the average net worth of the groups they come from, but also higher than the average personal net worth of Americans in general.[28]

If there is a reluctance to collect official data on the actual impact of preferential policies on the intended beneficiaries, it is virtually unthinkable politically to document the losses of those sacrificed to these policies. But the same economic logic that would suggest that the more fortunate members of the preferred groups are likely to gain most of the benefits would likewise suggest that the least fortunate members of the non-preferred groups are likely to suffer the greatest losses. Whether in jobs or college and university admissions, it is not the most outstanding performers who are likely to be displaced through preferential policies, but those who meet the standards with the least margin. A study of corporate executives in Bombay showed that the dominant group—the Gujaratis—experienced only a small decline, from 52 percent of all executives to 44 percent, after preferential programs brought Maharashtrians into the executive ranks for the first time. But the more modest proportions of Bombay executive positions held by people from South India—25 percent—was cut in half, to 12 percent.[29] Similar results appeared in the very different setting of pre-war Hungary, where preferential policies for Gentiles had little effect on the Jewish financial and industrial elite but had much more impact on the Jewish middle class and lower middle class.[30]

In countries such as the United States, where members of various racial, ethnic, and other groups overlap in their economic positions, to benefit the top of one group at the expense of the bottom of another group need not ameliorate economic inequalities, and may even increase them.

Part of the reason why the real beneficiaries and losers are difficult to identify is the practice of fraudulent identification for the sake of receiving preferences. Both in Indonesia and Malaysia, the term "Ali-Baba enterprises" has been coined to describe the widespread practice of having an indigenous "front man" (Ali) for a business that is in fact owned and operated by a Chinese (Baba).[31] Anti-Semitic policies in Poland during the interwar years similarly led some Jewish businesses to operate behind Gentile front men.[32] Decades later, under preferential policies in Kenya, Africans served as fronts for Asian-owned businesses.[33] Still later, fraudulent "minority" enterprises developed in the United States, in the wake of preferential programs for minority businessmen. American Indians (among others) are used as front men to get preferential treatment for supposedly minority-owned enterprises which are in fact owned and operated by non-minority people.[34]

THE ILLUSION OF COMPENSATION

What makes compensation an illusion is not only that sufferers are not in fact compensated, nor the effects of historic wrongs redressed—or even accurately identified and separated from innumerable other social factors at work simultaneously. Both the principle of compensation and the particular form of compensation via preferential policies require careful examination.

The Principle of Compensation

Given the mortality of human beings, often the only compensation for historic wrongs that is within the scope of our knowledge and control is purely symbolic compensation—taking from individuals who inflicted no harm and giving to individuals who suffered none. In addition to the moral shakiness and social dangers of such a policy, it also promotes a kind of social irredentism, a set of *a priori* grievances against living people, whether or not they have ever inflicted harm on those who feel aggrieved. Given the futile but bitter and bloody struggles engendered by territorial irredentism, there is little good to hope for by applying this same principle in a new field.

The factual reality that actual benefits from compensatory preferences tend to be concentrated in the already more fortunate elites among the preferred groups makes the moral case for such policies weaker and the social dangers greater. The more educated, articulate, and more politically sophisticated elites have every incentive to whip up group emotions in favor of more and better preferences, despite the increasing group polarization this may produce, and to be intransigent against any suggestion that any such preferences should ever be reduced or ended. This has been a common pattern in the most disparate settings.

In principle, compensation can take many forms, beginning with a simple transfer of money from one group to another. In practice, however, preferential policies are the form taken in many countries around the world. The implications of that particular form, and of its alternatives, raise still more troubling questions.

The Form of Compensation

If, notwithstanding all philosophic objections to the principle of group compensation, such a policy is in fact chosen, then the particular form of the compensation can make a major difference in the costs and the consequences of compensatory policies. When resources, or the benefits they create, are transferred from group A to group B, this is not necessarily—nor even likely—a zero-sum process, in which the value of what is lost by one is the same as the value of what is gained by the other. What is transferred may be subjectively valued differently by the losers and the recipients. There may also be objectively discernible differences in the use of the same resources by the two groups.

Compensatory policies may, in theory, take place through transfers of money, transfers of in-kind benefits, or through differential applications of rules and standards. In Australia, for example, various money and in-kind transfers to the aborigines add up to more than $2,000 annually for every aboriginal man, woman, and child.[35] Such transfers arouse relatively little political opposition or social backlash. Similarly, in the United States, monetary compensation for Japanese Americans interned during World War II aroused relatively little controversy—and even that little controversy quickly subsided, once the decision was made.

Such monetary transfers are less costly to individual members of the majority population the more the majority outnumbers the minority receiving the transfer. Obviously, if group A is 100 times as large as group B, each member of group B can receive $100 at a cost of only one dollar to each member of group A. However, even where the losses sustained by one group are significant, monetary transfers may still be efficient, in the narrowly economic sense that what is lost by one group as a whole is gained by another group, with no direct net loss to society as a whole. Whatever the merits or demerits of the particular transfer on other grounds, it is not inefficient. Politically and socially, the opposition to such transfers is therefore unlikely to be as great as opposition to the same net transfers in forms that cost more to the losers than is gained by the gainers. Preferential policies often cost the losers more than is gained by the gainers.

Preferential policies, by definition, involve a differential application of rules and standards to individuals originating in different groups. Even where the preferences are not stated in terms of differential rules or standards, but rather in terms of numerical quotas, "goals," or "targets," differences in the qualifications of the respective pools of applicants can readily make numerical similarities amount to differences in standards. This is a very common result in countries around the world. In Nigeria, for example, programs to have student populations reflect "the federal character" of the country—i.e., tribal quotas under regional names—led to a situation where cut-off scores for admission to the same college varied substantially between students from different tribes or regions.[36] In Sri Lanka, demographic "standardization" policies led to such a decline in student body qualifications as to provoke protests by academics, from whose hands these decisions were taken and vested in the Cabinet.[37] In India, attempts to meet quotas for untouchable students led to drastic reductions in the qualifications they needed for admission to various institutions.[38] Where applicant pools in different groups are different in qualifications, numerical quotas are equivalent to different standards. Therefore preferential policies in general, however phrased, are essentially an application of different rules or standards to individuals from different groups. The question then is: What are the effects of transfers between groups in this particular form?

There are many ways in which intergroup transfers through differential standards can become negative-sum processes, in which what is lost by one group exceeds what is gained by another, thus representing a direct loss to society as a whole—as well as causing indirect losses, due to a larger resistance or backlash than if the recipient group had obtained the same value or benefit in some other form. An obvious example is when a particular group, in which 90 percent of the students admitted to college succeed in graduating, loses places to another group in which only 30 percent of the students graduate. Group A must lose 900 graduates, in order for group B to gain 300 graduates. It might be objected that this overstates the net loss, since there may be some marginal benefit simply from having attended college, even without graduating. Offsetting this, however, is the fact that groups with lower qualifications tend to specialize in easier and less remunerative fields, whether in India, Malaysia, the Soviet Union, or the United States.[39] Therefore group A may lose 900 graduates largely concentrated in mathematics, science, and engineering, while group B gains 300 graduates largely concentrated in sociology, education, and ethnic studies.

The *apparent* losses to one group under preferential policies may also far exceed the real losses, thereby further raising the indirect social costs of backlash and turmoil. For example, an observer of India's preferential policies has commented:

> . . . we hear innumerable tales of persons being deprived of appointments in favour of people who ranked lower than they did in the relevant examinations. No doubt this does happen, but if all these people were, in fact, paying the price for

> appointments to Scheduled Castes, there would be many more SC persons appointed than there actually are. To illustrate: supposing that 300 people qualify for ten posts available. The top nine are appointed on merit but the tenth is reserved, so the authorities go down the list to find an SC applicant. They find one at 140 and he is appointed. Whereupon all 131 between him and the merit list feel aggrieved. He has not taken 131 posts; he has taken one, yet 131 people believe they have paid the price for it. Moreover, the remaining 159 often also resent the situation, believing that their chances were, somehow, lessened by the existence of SC reservations.[40]

Where certain opportunities are rigidly "set aside" for particular groups, in the sense that members of other groups cannot have them, even if these opportunities remain unused, then there is the potential for a maximum of grievance for a minimum of benefit transfer. Admission to medical school in India's state of Gujarat operates on this principle—and has led repeatedly to bloody riots in which many people have died.[41] Reservations or "set-asides" in general tend to provoke strong objections. The first major set-back for "affirmative action" in the U.S. Supreme Court was based on objections to reserved admissions places for minority applicants in the 1978 *Bakke* case.[42] A later major set-back occurred in *City of Richmond* v. *Croson* (1989), where minority business set-asides were struck down by the Supreme Court.[43] Similarly, in India, an exhaustive scholarly legal study of preferential policies found: "Virtually all of the litigation about compensatory discrimination has involved reservations, even though preferences in the form of provisions of facilities, resources, and protections directly affect a much larger number of recipients." This litigation has been initiated mostly by non-preferred individuals who complain of being adversely affected.[44] In some ultimate sense, non-preferred individuals are just as much adversely affected by preferences in other forms that direct resources away from them and toward preferred groups. But it is preference in the specific form of "reservation" or "set-aside" that seems most to provoke both violence and litigation.

By contrast, resource transfers designed to enable disadvantaged groups to meet standards are accepted while attempts to bring the standards down to them are overwhelmingly rejected. In the United States, preferential policies have repeatedly been rejected in public opinion polls. However, the same American public has strongly supported "special educational or vocational courses, free of charge, to enable members of minority groups to do better on tests." More than three-fifths of all whites even support "requiring large companies to set up special training programs for members of minority groups."[45] The issue is not simply whether one is for or against the advancement of particular groups or is willing to see transfers of resources for their betterment. The method by which their betterment is attempted matters greatly in terms of whether such efforts have the support or the opposition of others.

CHAPTER SEVEN

REPLACING ILLUSIONS

With all the empirical weaknesses, logical flaws, and social dangers of preferential policies, why have they become so popular and spread so rapidly around the world? One reason is that their *political* attractions are considerable. They offer an immediate response—a quick fix—at relatively little government expense, to the demands of vocal, aroused, and often organized elites, speaking in the name of restive masses. This restiveness of the masses is by no means incidental. Violence has frequently preceded preferences, from the South African mines in the early twentieth century to the American ghetto riots of the 1960s to the Malay and Indonesian riots against the Chinese, threats and terrorism in Assam and Bombay, and the massive mob violence against the Tamils in Sri Lanka. This violence by the masses is typically used politically to promote elite purposes via preferential policies. An international study of ethnic conflicts concluded:

> Preferences tend to respond to middle-class aspirations almost entirely. They do little or nothing about the resentments of those who do not aspire to attend secondary school or university, to enter the modern private sector or the bureaucracy, or

> to become businessmen. Although lower-class resentments are often profound—it is not, after all, the middle class that typically participates in ethnic violence—the resentments may have nothing to do with occupational mobility and preferences do not address them.[1]

In short, preferential policies are politically attractive as a response, however socially ineffective or counterproductive such policies may later prove to be in practice. At a sufficiently superficial level, the moral attractions of preferential policies are considerable as well. Even in South Africa, moral appeals were made on behalf of a "civilized labor policy"—protecting European workers' customary standard of living from being undercut by Africans and Indians accustomed to living on less—and clergy, intellectuals, and others not personally benefiting joined in support of these policies on that basis. Preferential policies allow intellectuals as well as politicians to be on the side of the angels (as locally defined at the time) at low cost—or rather, at a low down payment, for the real costs come later, and have sometimes been paid in blood.

The last refuge of a failed policy is "the long run," in which it will supposedly be a success. In other words, those who predicted the short run wrongly ask to be trusted with the much harder task of predicting the long run rightly. This argument, used to defend the counterproductive effects of preferential policies, is far less defensible in an international perspective where older preferential policies (as in India or Sri Lanka) have progressed from intergroup political hostility to bloodshed in the streets and deaths by the hundreds, while newer programs (as in the United States) are still in the process of increasing group polarization and the even more recent preferential policies taking shape in Australia and New Zealand are still at the stage of optimistic predictions.

Even the most damning indictment of a policy is almost

certain to be met with the response: "But what would you replace it with?" However effective as a political tactic, such a question confuses rather than clarifies. It is like an arbitrary prohibition against saying that the emperor has no clothes, until a complete wardrobe has been designed. The question misconceives policy, and human actions in general, in yet another way: No one who extinguishes a forest fire or removes a cancer has to "replace" it with anything. We are well rid of evils.

This is not to say that none of the aspects of social issues raised during "affirmative action" controversies should ever be addressed by public policy. The case for public policy in general, or for a particular public policy, must be made on the individual merits of the particular issues raised—but not as a general "replacement" for some discredited policy.

What must be replaced are the social illusions and misconceptions underlying preferential policies, for any alternative policy based on the same illusions and misconceptions will have the same fatal weaknesses in its structure. In some countries and for some purposes, social policy may wish to ameliorate the lot of the less fortunate or make it possible for individuals or groups to acquire the knowledge and skills necessary for their own advancement. It is infinitely more important that such efforts be based on facts and logic than that there be one particular scheme selected from innumerable possibilities as the uniquely designated "replacement" for existing policy.

We may or may not be able to agree on what the ideal, or even a viable, policy must be. What we can agree on is far more fundamental: We can agree to *talk sense.* That will mean abandoning a whole vocabulary of political rhetoric which pre-empts factual questions by arbitrarily calling statistical disparities "discrimination," "exclusion," "segregation," and the like. It will mean confronting issues instead of impugning motives. It will mean that goals have to be specified and those specifics defended, rather than speaking in terms of seeking some nebulously unctuous "change" or "social justice." Perhaps more than anything else, talking sense will mean that policies must be examined in terms of the incentives they create, and the results to which these incentives lead, rather than the hopes they embody. It will mean that evidence must take precedence over assertion and reiteration.

INCENTIVES VERSUS HOPES

"Temporary" Preferences

Many of the factual findings of this study will be surprising to many only because incentives have not usually been the focus of discussions of preferential policies. For example, given the incentives, it can hardly be surprising that preferential policies do not become temporary merely because their proponents use the word "temporary." The incentives are to do exactly what has been done, in country after country: extend and expand both the preferences and the list of beneficiaries, not to mention those individuals who make themselves beneficiaries through fraud.

Once we face up to the fact that "temporary" preferences are not likely to be temporary in fact, and that the group whose history provides the moral rationale for initiating preferential policies is unlikely to remain the sole group preferred in a multi-ethnic society, then we must abandon the make-believe issues that are debated under the false assumption of temporary preferences for a particular group. The real issue then becomes: What are the likely consequences of an enduring policy of group preferences for the whole range of groups that are likely to get them? The answer to that question will depend, not on what rationales there are for preferences, but rather on what *incentives* these policies create—including incentives for members of the preferred group, for members of other groups likely to seek preferences, for members of groups likely to resent and react to preferences, and for a whole group-consciousness industry that acquires a vested interest in agitating emotional issues in an ever more tense, polarized, and even explosive atmosphere.

The moral issue is then no longer whether group A or B deserves compensatory preferences, but whether groups C, D, E, etc., also deserve such preferences—especially if these latter groups are larger, more educated, or otherwise better positioned to use the preferences, thereby diluting or destroying the value of preferences for group A or B, who may have stronger moral claims or more urgent social needs. As the case of untouchables in India and blacks in the United States both illustrate, it is all too easy for a tragically unfortunate group of people to be used simply as an entering wedge to create benefits going largely to others in much more fortunate circumstances, whether those others are within their own racial or social group or numerous outsiders to whom the preferential principle is successively extended. Clearly, no recitation of the historic oppressions suffered by blacks can justify preferences for white, middle-class women, whom some believe to be the principal beneficiaries of the acceptance of the preferential principle.[2]

Both in India and in the United States, a point is ultimately reached where the initially designated beneficiaries of preferential policies begin to object to the continued extension of that status to others. Blacks, for example, objected to legislation in the Louisiana House of Representatives which extended "minority" status to Cajuns.[3] In India, untouchable leader Dr. B. R. Ambedkar fought successfully against the extension of central government preferences to members of the "other backward classes" in the Indian constitution.[4]

An analysis of preferential policies in terms of the incentives they create cannot treat preferences as simply a benefit added to existing social processes. Preferential policies change the very nature of processes—whether these be hiring processes, college admissions processes, or other social processes. An employer who was once free to choose among job applicants on the basis of his own assessments of their ability to do the job must, after preferential policies, consider also how readily his decision can be justified to third parties, in terms that will be understood and accepted by those who are less knowledgeable about his business, who were not present at the interview, and who would have less experience on which to base an assessment such as he made. "Objective" criteria in general and educational credentials in particular are likely to gain more weight under these circumstances because third parties can understand such things, even if other qualities are in fact more important on the job. The growth of credentialism can further disadvantage less fortunate groups, especially if preferences have also been extended to other groups with more credentials—e.g., middle-class white women in America as compared to black males. There can be *fewer* job opportunities for less educated black males after preferential policies that extend far beyond them to encompass groups better able to play the game under the new rules.

Where preferential policies apply not only to the initial intake (hiring, college admissions) but also to subsequent progress (promotions, college grades, honors), the incentives created can operate at cross-purposes. For example, the requirement that initial intake numbers be reported to third parties tends, by itself, to create incentives to hire more of the designated group. However, the knowledge that this group's subsequent progress must also be reported—and can become the basis for costly litigation and large damage awards—inhibits the hiring of individuals from the preferred group, unless they seem more "safe" than individuals who can be readily demoted or terminated because they come from groups without legal preferences. Which of these contending tendencies will predominate in the actual decisions can vary with the industry or activity, the nature of the pools of applicants, the policies and practices of the third-party observers, and whether the decision-maker is spending his own money or the taxpayers' money. The point here is that, once more, the changes in the nature of the process induced by preferential processes need not increase the opportunities of the officially preferred group—and may, on net balance, *reduce* those opportunities. Where the existence of preferential policies also leads to a slackening of efforts among the preferred group, then the dangers of counterproductive results are further increased.

Abstract possibilities of counterproductive results from preferential policies are by no means conclusive. However, they do make it easier to understand empirical patterns observed in the United States, India, and Malaysia, where the poorer members of the preferred group have actually *retrogressed* during the same span of time when the group's elite has advanced dramatically. Preferential policies unequivocally create an increased demand for the "safe" and credentialed members of the preferred group, while making the less educated, less skilled, and less experienced members a more risky gamble for an employer than they would be in the absence of preferences. This is especially so in the United States, where preferences are predicated on prior discrimination and on continuing dangers of discrimination, with statistical disparities often being equated with such discrimination in courts of law, which can make multi-million-dollar damage awards to those judged to be victims.

Evasions of Preferences

Given the differing costs of discrimination to those in government who impose preferential policies and those businessmen in the private sector who are required to carry them out, it can hardly be surprising that both opposition and evasions have been aroused against such policies in country after country. Where circumstances bring economic considerations to the fore among political leaders, as during the Thirty Years War in the seventeenth century or during Catherine the Great's attempts to advance the backward Russian economy in the eighteenth century, then these rulers themselves have either openly or surreptitiously reversed discriminatory policies.

In the absence of an understanding of incentives, explanations tend to attribute evasion or opposition to preferential policies to a hostility to the particular groups designated as beneficiaries of these policies. Clearly this cannot explain widespread white evasions of policies designed to help whites, as in South Africa. Once the *multiple* sources of resistance to preferential policies are admitted, it is no longer possible to attribute automatically the failures of such policies to "institutional racism," "unconscious bias," or similar explanations, *without evidence.* Circular reasoning cannot substitute for evidence.

Incentives allow discussions to proceed in terms of the actual decision-makers involved, individual or institutional, seeking their own specific self-interest rather than in terms of some arbitrarily collectivized "society," "power structure," or other such construct not corresponding to any empirically demonstrable decision-making unit. The poetic license of speaking of "society" as acting this way or that is a declaration of intellectual bankruptcy, as far as empirical evidence is concerned. Such metaphors are an evasion of crucial questions about incentives and causation.

Incentives of Activists

Unelected "spokesmen" who speak boldly to the media in the name of groups seeking or receiving preferential policies are a common social phenomenon from New Zealand to Britain to North America. There are also common patterns in their pronouncements, reflecting common incentives facing them. Any fundamental re-examination of the assumptions behind preferential policies—and still more so, any resulting change of policies—can expect to encounter their vocal, bitter, and determined opposition, including inevitable charges of racism against outsiders, labels of "traitor" put on any members of their own group who disagree publicly with them, and whatever other claims or charges seem likely to be politically effective.

The common thread of group activists around the world is separatism. Insofar as their group, whether a majority or a minority, reaches a modus vivendi with other groups, there is less of a role for group activists. Accordingly, group activists often seek separate languages, separate institutions, and even separate territories. Even where most of the group already speaks the language of the surrounding society, as among the Maoris of New Zealand, group activists seek to artificially reconstitute a separate language community. In Australia, all-aborigines schools have been established, emphasizing the teaching of the aboriginal languages.[5]

Unrealizable demands are another common feature of group activists, whether these demands are for massive "reparations" payments for slavery for blacks in the United States or making the Maori language the official language of New Zealand.[6] While demands that can be met might benefit the group, demands that cannot be met benefit the group activist. The point is "to create the appropriate climate for bitter recriminations," as an observer of Australian aboriginal activists put it.[7] Sometimes, through miscalculation, a demand may be made that can be and is met—in which case, what is conceded must then be denounced as paltry and insultingly inadequate, however important it may have been depicted as being when it seemed unattainable.

Threats of catastrophe if their demands are not met are another common tactic of group activists. An aboriginal activist in Australia described the aborigines as being of a radically different culture, as "totally frustrated and angry with white society," so that unless whites get rid of their "inbuilt bias and prejudice," he predicted "there's going to be an absolute disaster in Australia." He concluded: "We've got to find alternative principles if humanity is to survive."[8] By contrast, one of the few aborigines actually *elected* by aborigines depicted his people as sharing many of the values and aspirations of white Australians, offered no such apocalyptic view of the future, and declared that many of the activists' ideas were foreign to aboriginal culture, though congenial to "the trendy middle classes."[9]

A key factor in the success of vocal activists around the world is their ability to strike a responsive chord in the "trendy middle classes" in the name of a group which has not elected them and which often has views radically different from theirs. Such activists are not "leaders" of their people in any meaningful sense. That fact can only become more painfully clear if a fundamental change in public policy makes the internal development of the group the prime focus. In such a situation today's group activists would have little role to play except that of attempting to discredit or sabotage the effort. They may be politically very formidable in that role, however.

PRESUMPTIONS VERSUS PEOPLE

Except in the case of majority preferences in majority economies, preferential policies are intended to favor groups currently "under-represented" in desirable occupations or institutions. Both majorities in minority economies and minorities in majority economies have equated statistical inequalities with moral inequities. In extreme cases—not necessarily rare cases—the presumption that groups would be evenly represented in various sectors and levels of society, in the absence of discrimination, has become a belief almost hermetically sealed off from any logical or empirical argument. Criticism is dismissed as malevolently motivated, evidence as culturally biased, criteria as irrelevant.

Evidence that clearly contradicts the vision has often been hidden by redefinition. For example, where the assumption is that non-whites' lower economic position is due to whites' discrimination, non-white groups who have been successful in the same society are an obvious embarrassment to the proponents of this theory. In Britain, this has led to a redefinition of all non-white groups, including Asians, as "black."[10] Thus Asians disappear as a separate group by verbal sleight-of-hand, as the collective economic, educational, and other performances of "blacks" as a whole are compared to those of whites. In the United States, a similar burying of discordant evidence is achieved by using the ponderous phrase "people of color" to encompass all non-whites, thereby swamping the above-average income statistics of Chinese and Japanese Americans under the larger numbers of below-average income statistics from blacks and other low-income, non-white groups. In Canada, the lumping-together phrase is "visible minorities." It too helps conceal the fact that some non-white groups in Canada are more prosperous than some white groups. The particular words used to lump disparate groups together differ from country to country but the tactic is the same.

In short, no matter what the evidence says, the vision is protected from it. Such heads-I-win-and-tails-you-lose arguments have become as commonplace among group activists in Britain as in the United States.[11] Implicit in this vision is the assumption that the respective pools of potential group "representatives" are not substantially different or that the differences are not relevant. This assumption is contradicted by objective evidence from around the world as to the large variations—both qualitative and quantitative—in educational achievement between groups in the same society, whether India, Israel, Sri Lanka, Nigeria, Malaysia, or the United States.

Non-quantifiable differences are not necessarily any less important factors in statistical disparities, though such differences are often dismissed as "stereotypes." However, so-called "stereotypes" about group behavior often show a certain consistency between what group members say about themselves and what others say about them, though the connotations may differ. Many backward groups from Burma to Guyana "view themselves as the major obstacle to their own advancement."[12] Nor can these be dismissed as brain-washed minorities, full of "self-hate." Majorities in charge of their own preferential programs have also confronted their own behavior as factors inhibiting the progress they wish to make. This was perhaps nowhere more candidly stated than in an official Malaysian government publication concerning the economic problems of the indigenous Malays or Bumiputera:

> The history of Bumiputera has also indicated that the mere ownership and control of resources without proper and necessary skills and initiative have led to the gradual erosion and eventual loss of ownership and control over the important resources such as the tin bearing land. The willingness to farm out the wealth to others and to derive income from tributes from the tin mining land has passed on substantial benefits of the wealth to other interests. The practice of assigning to others for specific remuneration the use of licenses granted to them has not enabled some Bumiputera to participate actively in the economic activities for which the licenses were issued. Such inclinations reflect an unwillingness

> to work and take risks to maximize the wealth that can be gained from the possession and effective use of licenses. In addition, such inclinations will not lead to an improvement in the ability of Bumiputera to manage money and business. The quick disposal of the shares of companies to realize short-term financial gains further indicates an over-concentration on short-term financial benefits rather than a willingness to realize further the long-term potentials from holding on to the financial assets. Idle land owned by Bumiputera in choice locations in urban areas, for example, in Kampung Baharu in the Federal Territory, or the failure to use the land to its maximum advantages in the construction of urban properties also indicates a failure to maximize fully and manage successfully the wealth of Bumiputera. These practices have contributed to the impoverishment of Bumiputera and will impede the further accumulation of wealth of the community if these trends persist and are not arrested. These attitudes and other constraints to the wealth accumulation, therefore must be overcome if the socio-economic position of Bumiputera is to be further improved.[13]

In the very different setting of Hungary, half a century ago, group differences in skills and attitudes were likewise admitted by a leader of the majority as an explanation of why a minority so dramatically outperformed them, despite majority preferential policies. On October 10, 1940, Hungary's long-time regent, Admiral Miklós Horthy, wrote to the Prime Minister:

> As regards the Jewish problem, I have been an anti-Semite through all my life. I have never had

> contact with Jews. I have considered it intolerable that here in Hungary every factory, bank, large fortune, business, theatre, press, commercial enterprise, etc., should be in the hands of Jews, and that Jews should be the image reflected of Hungary, especially abroad. Since, however, one of the most important tasks of the government is to raise the living standards (*i.e.*, we have to acquire wealth), it is impossible, in a year or two, to eliminate the Jews, who have everything in their hands, and to replace them by incompetent, mostly unworthy big-mouth elements, for we would become bankrupt. This requires a generation at least.[14]

Surely Malays and Hungarian Gentiles are not the only people on this planet whose own behavior patterns have been among the factors inhibiting their progress. Yet any such candid recitation of such patterns among many other groups in other countries would automatically be denounced as "blaming the victim"—not only by political activists but even by scholars. Any suggestion of difficulties in finding qualified members of any group for any job is likely to be dismissed as a lame excuse, even in courts of law. In the United States, the unbridled vilification of the Moynihan Report in 1965 marked virtually the beginning of the end of candid discussions of minority groups. Ironically, the Moynihan Report was a plea for more government help for blacks, and what it said had already been said by black scholars, including some who joined in the vilification of Moynihan. Moreover, the candor of the Moynihan Report did not begin to approach the painful frankness of *Black Bourgeoisie* by E. Franklin Frazier, the outstanding black sociologist.

Any policy that attempts to advance the interests of any group in any country must begin with the reality of their situation—not with hermetically sealed visions that offer psychic comfort or politically useful illusions benefiting a relative handful of elite or activist individuals. It is far more important to understand what a viable policy must be based on than to narrow arbitrarily the range of such possible policies to one specified "solution."

Denial of any group's internal problems can mean denying a history of long and sometimes heroic efforts to overcome those problems. The role of the Catholic Church in socially uplifting the Irish in America[15] is just one of these historic efforts leading to the social transformation of a people. Both blacks and whites participated in successful efforts to develop an educated class among blacks in the first generation after slavery and on into the twentieth century.[16] The "Jewish Enlightenment" in Europe and the spectacular rise of the Scots in the eighteenth century are other examples of a kind of valuable human experience that is often ignored today because to admit that there were internal problems in the first place would shatter the hermetically sealed vision.

One symptom of the determined refusal to examine the characteristics of a group nominated for preferences is the setting of numerical "goals" *without the slightest mention* of the size of the pool of qualified people from whom these goals are to be met. Where the problem of pool size is even obliquely acknowledged, it is often in the context of establishing numerical goals for the pool itself—which simply pushes the same issue back one stage. Ultimately, this logically leads back to childhood and the values of the home and the group. When Maori students, admitted under preferential policies at New Zealand's University of Auckland, fail to show up for tutorials as often as other students,[17] their academic failures cannot be attributed automatically to institutional racism or to not having enough "role models"—not if the purpose is to advance Maoris rather than to score ideological points.

POLITICS VERSUS PROGRESS

The ingredients of political success and the ingredients of social progress are not only different but often antithetical. Nothing was more politically successful than the preferential policies which led Sri Lanka into race riots, atrocities, and civil war. Even Marxist parties, ideologically opposed to ethnic group preferences, were forced by electoral disasters to advocate such policies as the price of political survival. Preferential policies in Pakistan were politically robust enough to survive and flourish after their initial beneficiary group, the East Bengalis, seceded to form the separate nation of Bangladesh. Preferential policies in Nigeria began before independence and survived in varying forms through changes in constitutions, military coups, and a civil war that took over a million lives. The political success of preferential policies in Guyana, India, and Malaysia has likewise been impressive.

What has been far less impressive is the social record of preferential policies. However beneficial to the elites of preferred groups, such policies have helped raise the masses from poverty to prosperity only in South Africa, where the once urgent "poor white" problem among the Afrikaners has been solved by the ruthless sacrifice of the interests of the vastly larger non-white population and the relentless suppression of their resistance. Yet it is by no means clear that the long-run costs of this social "success" will prove to be worth it, even for South African whites, many of whom have begun emigrating to other countries, in anticipation of trouble in the years ahead.

The reasons for the political success of preferential policies highlight the political difficulties of alternative policies designed to enable genuinely unfortunate people to advance. Preferential policies allow large promises about the future to be made by politicians at small immediate cost to the government. Such policies reward vocal leaders of the preferred groups by creating benefits focused on their class and flatter the group as a whole that its problems are caused by other people, whose wrong-doing or unfair advantages will be suppressed by government. This approach fits in neatly with various "liberation" themes, whose essential message is that other people are to blame for one's troubles. With the complex difficulties and painful trade-offs involved in social advancement reduced to the simple level of group conflict, the issue can be presented politically and its goals defined in terms politically comprehensible to all. Conflict has obvious media appeal as well and moralists and intellectuals can choose the side considered to be that of the angels. Politicians benefit by gaining the political support of the beneficiary groups. Where those groups do not constitute a majority, then the preferential policies can nevertheless succeed politically by keeping a low profile, by being redefined as anti-discrimination efforts, or by being justified by such moral rationales as will mollify the majority.

Consider, by contrast, the political situation facing a program which genuinely intends to aid the advancement of less fortunate people by improving those people's education, skills, and habits. Such a program must take far more time, probably cost far more money, and cannot provide either the group conflict so useful to the media or the sense of moral superiority so much in demand by crusaders or others who want to be on the side of the angels. The scope and pace of genuine advancement for less fortunate masses cannot produce as dramatic results as a doubling or tripling of group members in a few elite positions within a few years under preferential policies. If thousands more minority women who might have become maids become secretaries instead, that is still not as dramatic as having three minority Cabinet members instead of one, even though far more people would be benefited by the former, including people far more in need of help. Politically, symbolic representation in visible high-level positions "sells." Preferential policies can deliver that better and faster than any policy of helping less fortunate masses advance. Most important of all, it can deliver before the next election.

Education is widely recognized as a key factor in the advancement of individuals and groups. Whether in India or the United States or in other countries, the tendency is to focus efforts at the visible, high-level end of education—at the colleges and universities, including post-graduate education. Obviously, the genuinely less fortunate seldom reach these levels. If they are to be helped, the help must come much earlier in the educational process and the task will be infinitely more difficult than lowering admissions standards in higher education to achieve statistical representation. Moreover, the struggle will not be the kind of struggle between groups, or between good and evil, that the media can dramatize but instead a harder, slower, and less glamorous struggle between the inherent requirements of quality education and the habits, attitudes, and beliefs of people who have not had to deal with such requirements before. School disrupters will have to be dealt with as problems to be gotten rid of, rather than as victims to be defended by in-group organizations or "public interest" lawyers from the general society.

Even assuming that all of these educational difficulties can be overcome and high-quality students begin to emerge from the system, they will not emerge from high school for another 12 years, from college for 16 years, or from post-graduate education and professional apprenticeship levels for 20 years. Such time spans are simply beyond the horizon for politicians whose focus is the next election. Genuine educational improvement is at a clear disadvantage politically in competing with preferential policies that can offer a "quick fix" before the voters go to the polls. Even if there are early signs that a program is starting to work, rising test scores in Harlem elementary schools will never carry the same political weight as appointing a few more high-level minority officials or even increasing the number of minority students admitted to the city's colleges and universities without meeting the standards required of others.

Perhaps some judicious blend of preferential programs and programs designed to improve the performances of less educated groups might be attempted, but the two kinds of programs create incentives that work at cross-purposes, even if their goals are the same. Forcing students to meet higher standards—a painful process for them and their teachers alike—will be made all the more difficult if the students know that these standards are unnecessary for them to reach whatever educational or employment goals they have, or even to be promoted to the next grade. If group representation statistics are the standard by which institutions will be judged, other standards will be sacrificed for the sake of body count. This is true not only of educational institutions but of other institutions as well.

Political feasibility is the greatest obstacle to new policies with an over-riding goal of advancing the less fortunate because time is the key ingredient in such advancement on a large scale. Even in the extreme case of South Africa, where massive transfers of the nation's resources were focused on a small minority of its people, in *addition* to preferential policies pursued in utter disregard of the losses and even tragedies suffered by others as a result, it was decades before the Afrikaner "poor whites" became middle class. Only in terms of political appearances are preferential policies a "quick fix." The dangers of an actual retrogression among the masses of the beneficiary group cannot be dismissed, either from an analytical or an empirical perspective. Even greater dangers have materialized in countries that have experienced bloodshed in the wake of group polarization brought on by preferential policies.

Replacing Illusions

While current political feasibility may be the touchstone of the professional politician, it cannot be the last word for others. In many countries, what is most politically feasible is a continued drift in the direction of group polarization and the dangers and disasters this entails. Specific alternative policies will differ for different groups and different countries. What is crucial is that these alternatives be examined in terms of the *incentives* they create and the results to which such incentives can be expected to lead—regardless of the rationales, aspirations, or symbolism of these policies. Determining in this way what *should* be done is not an exercise in Utopianism, for once there is a consensus on what needs to be done, that in itself changes what is politically feasible.

NOTES

Chapter 1: Patterns

1. Walter Block, "Economic Intervention, Discrimination, and Unforeseen Consequences," *Discrimination, Affirmative Action, and Equal Opportunity,* edited by W. E. Block and M. A. Walker (Vancouver: The Fraser Institute, 1982), p. 111.
2. See *Economic Report of the President* (Washington: U.S. Government Printing Office, 1973), p. 105.

Chapter 2: Majority Preferences in Majority Economies

1. Jennifer Roback, "The Political Economy of Segregation: The Case of Segregated Streetcars," *Journal of Economic History,* December 1986, pp. 899, 907, 909, 913, 914.
2. *Ibid.*, p. 914.
3. *Ibid.*, pp. 909, 910.
4. *Ibid.*, pp. 899, 904, 905.
5. *Ibid.*, pp. 913–914.
6. *Ibid.*, pp. 914–915.
7. Sarah Gordon, *Hitler, Germans, and the "Jewish Question"* (Princeton: Princeton University Press, 1984), pp. 168–169, 177.

8. Louis Wirth, *The Ghetto* (Chicago: University of Chicago Press, 1956), p. 229.
9. Merle Lipton, *Capitalism and Apartheid: South Africa, 1910–84* (Totowa, New Jersey: Rowman and Littlefield, 1985), p. 112.
10. *Ibid.*
11. *Ibid.*, p. 113.
12. George M. Fredrickson, *White Supremacy: A Comparative Study in American and South African History* (New York: Oxford University Press, 1981), p. 232.
13. Harold D. Nelson, editor, *South Africa: A Country Study* (Washington: U.S. Government Printing Office, 1981), p. 36.
14. Merle Lipton, *Capitalism and Apartheid,* p. 19.
15. *Ibid.*, p. 239.
16. *Ibid.*, pp. 19–20; George M. Fredrickson, *White Supremacy,* p. 233.
17. Charles H. Young and Helen R. Reid, *The Japanese Canadians* (Toronto: University of Toronto Press, 1938), pp. 49–50.
18. Merle Lipton, *Capitalism and Apartheid,* p. 39.
19. Abedian and B. Standish, "Poor Whites and the Role of the State: The Evidence," *South African Journal of Economics,* June 1985, p. 143.
20. Merle Lipton, *Capitalism and Apartheid,* p. 42.
21. *Ibid.*, p. 146.
22. *Ibid.*, pp. 152–153.
23. *Ibid.*, p. 209.
24. Harold D. Nelson, *South Africa,* pp. xiv, 227.
25. Heibert Adam and Hermann Giliomee, *The Rise and Crisis of Afrikaner Power* (Cape Town: David Phillip, 1979), p. 174.
26. Abedian and B. Standish, "Poor Whites and the Role of the State: The Evidence," *South African Journal of Economics,* June 1985, p. 144.
27. *Ibid.*, p. 148.
28. *Ibid.*, pp. 141–165.
29. Merle Lipton, *Capitalism and Apartheid,* p. 9.

30. *Ibid.*, Chapters 3, 6; Craig Charney, "Class Conflict and the National Party Split," *Journal of Southern African Studies,* April 1984, pp. 269–282; Heibert Adam and Hermann Giliomee, *The Rise and Crisis of Afrikaner Power,* pp. 177–184.
31. Brian Lapping, *Apartheid: A History* (New York: George Braziller, 1987), p. 164.
32. See Jonathan I. Israel, *European Jewry in the Age of Mercantilism* (Oxford: The Clarendon Press, 1985), pp. 27, 28, 166.
33. *Ibid.*, pp. 16–18, 72–73.
34. Paul Johnson, *A History of the Jews* (New York: Harper & Row, 1987), p. 243.
35. Jonathan I. Israel, *European Jewry in the Age of Mercantilism,* pp. 73–74.
36. *Ibid.*, Chapter V.
37. *Ibid.*, pp. 89, 93.
38. *Ibid.*, pp. 86, 89.
39. *Ibid.*, p. 88.
40. *Ibid.*, p. 87.
41. See, for example, Gilbert Osofsky, *Harlem: The Making of a Ghetto* (New York: Harper & Row, 1966), Chapter 8.
42. *Ibid.*, p. 117.
43. Jeffrey S. Gurock, *When Harlem Was Jewish, 1870–1930* (New York: Columbia University Press, 1979), p. 148.
44. E. Franklin Frazier, *The Negro in the United States* (New York: The Macmillan Company, 1971), pp. 262–264.
45. See, for example, St. Clair Drake and Horace R. Clayton, *Black Metropolis: A Student Negro Life in a Northern City* (New York: Harcourt, Brace & World, Inc., 1970), Vol. 1, p. 185; Olivier Zunz, *The Changing Face of Inequality: Urbanization, Industrial Development and Immigrants in Detroit, 1880–1920* (Chicago: University of Chicago Press, 1982), p. 375; Kenneth L. Kusmer, *A Ghetto Takes Shape: Black Cleveland, 1870–1930* (Urbana: University of Illinois Press, 1978), pp. 165–167.
46. See, for example, Gilbert Osofsky, *Harlem: The Making of a Ghetto,* p. 110.

47. See Thomas Sowell, *Race and Economics* (New York: David McKay Co., 1975), pp. 166–168.
48. Roger P. Bartlett, *Human Capital: The Settlement of Foreigners in Russia 1762–1804* (Cambridge: Cambridge University Press, 1979), p. 87.

Chapter 3: Majority Preferences in Minority Economies

1. Donald L. Horowitz, *Ethnic Groups in Conflict* (Berkeley: University of California Press, 1985), pp. 176–177.
2. *Ibid.*, p. 153.
3. Thomas Sowell, *Ethnic America* (New York: Basic Books, 1981), p. 123; G. Cresciani, "Italian Emigrants 1920–1945," *The Australian People,* edited by James Jupp (North Ryde, Australia: Angus Robertson Publishers, 1988), p. 610.
4. Victor Purcell, *The Chinese in Southeast Asia,* 2nd edition (Kuala Lumpur: Oxford University Press, 1980), pp. 277–279.
5. Mohamed Suffian bin Hashim, "Problems and Issues of Higher Education Development in Malaysia," *Development of Higher Education in Southeast Asia: Problems and Issues,* ed. Yip Yat Hoong (Singapore: Regional Institute of Higher Education and Development, 1973), p. 64.
6. Donald L. Horowitz, *Ethnic Groups in Conflict,* p. 178.
7. *Ibid.*, pp. 172–173.
8. *Ibid.*, p. 657.
9. Mahatir bin Mohamad, *The Malay Dilemma* (Kuala Lumpur: Federal Publications, 1970), p. 21.
10. *Ibid.*, p. 25.
11. Thomas Sowell, *The Economics and Politics of Race* (New York: William Morrow & Co., 1983), p. 24.
12. *Mid-Term Review of the Second Malaysia Plan, 1971–75* (Kuala Lumpur: The Government Press, 1973), p. 81.
13. Mohamed Suffian bin Hashim, "Problems and Issues of Higher Education Development in Malaysia," *Development of*

Higher Education in Southeast Asia, ed. Yip Yat Hoong, Table 8, pp. 63, 64.

14. *Ibid.*, pp. 70–71.
15. Bee-lan Chan Wang, "Governmental Intervention in Ethnic Stratification: Effects of the Distribution of Students Among Fields of Study," *Comparative Education Review,* February 1977, p. 110.
16. *Mid-Term Review of the Second Malaysia Plan, 1971–1975,* pp. 76, 78.
17. *Ibid.*, p. 85.
18. Tai Yoke Lin, "Ethnic Restructuring in Malaysia, 1979–80: The Employment Perspective," *From Independence to Statehood: Managing Ethnic Conflict in Five African and Asian States,* ed. Robert B. Goldmann and A. Jeyaratnam Wilson (London: Frances Pinter, 1984), p. 48.
19. *Ibid.*, p. 50.
20. *Fourth Malaysia Plan, 1981–1985* (Kuala Lumpur: The National Printing Department, 1981), p. 349.
21. *Ibid.*, p. 352.
22. *Ibid.*, p. 349.
23. Mavis Puthucheary, "Public Policies Relating to Business and Land, and the Impact on Ethnic Relations in Peninsular Malaysia," *From Independence to Statehood,* ed. Robert B. Goldmann and A. Jeyaratnam Wilson, p. 163.
24. Lim Mah Hui, "The Ownership and Control of Large Corporations in Malaysia: The Role of Chinese Businessmen," *The Chinese in Southeast Asia,* editors Peter Gosling and Linda Y. C. Lim (Singapore: Maruzen Asia, 1983), pp. 281, 284, 308.
25. Mavis Puthucheary, "Public Policies Relating to Business and Land," *From Independence to Statehood,* ed. Robert B. Goldmann and A. Jeyaratnam Wilson, p. 158.
26. *Ibid.*, p. 164.
27. Mahatir bin Mohamad, *The Malay Dilemma,* p. 44.
28. Donald R. Snodgrass, *Inequality and Economic Development in Malaysia* (Kuala Lumpur: Oxford University Press, 1980),

p. 82; Robert Klitgaard and Ruth Katz, "Overcoming Ethnic Inequalities: Lessons for Malaysia," *Journal of Policy Analysis and Management,* Vol. 2, No. 3 (1983), pp. 335, 343; Pang Eng Fong, "Race, Income Distribution, and Development in Malaysia and Singapore," *The Chinese in Southeast Asia,* edited by Linda Y. C. Lim and L. A. Peter Gosling (Singapore: Maruzen Asia, 1983), Vol. 1, p. 321.

29. *Fourth Malaysia Plan,* p. 79; *Fifth Malaysia Plan,* p. 134.
30. *Fourth Malaysia Plan,* p. 350.
31. *Fifth Malaysia Plan,* pp. 489–490.
32. *Ibid.*, pp. 490–491.
33. *Ibid.*, 489.
34. Computed from *Fifth Malaysia Plan,* p. 104.
35. *Ibid.*, p. 105.
36. Geoffrey Moorhouse, *India Britannica* (New York: Harper & Row, 1983), p. 248.
37. Richard F. Nyrop, et al., *Area Handbook for India* (Washington, D.C.: U.S. Government Printing Office, 1975), p. 127.
38. *Ibid.*, p. 128.
39. *Ibid.*, p. 140.
40. Myron Weiner, *Sons of the Soil: Migration and Ethnic Conflict in India* (Princeton: Princeton University Press, 1978), pp. 49–59.
41. *Ibid.*, p. 19.
42. Lelah Dushkin, "Backward Class Benefits and Social Class in India, 1920–1970," *Economic and Political Weekly,* April 7, 1979, p. 661.
43. D. L. Sheth, "Reservations Policy Revisited," *Economic and Political Weekly,* November 14, 1987, p. 1957.
44. Myron Weiner, *Sons of the Soil,* pp. 79–80; Richard F. Nyrop, et al., *Area Handbook for India,* p. 128.
45. Myron Weiner and Mary Fainsod Katzenstein, *India's Preferential Policies: Migrants, The Middle Classes, and Ethnic Equality* (Chicago: University of Chicago Press, 1981), p. 95.
46. Myron Weiner, *Sons of the Soil,* p. 102.
47. *Ibid.*, pp. 88–89.
48. *Ibid.*
49. Amalendo Guha, "Colonisation of Assam: Second Phase

1840–1859," *The Indian Economic and Social History Review*, December 1961, p. 292.

50. Myron Weiner, *Sons of the Soil*, p. 78.
51. *Ibid.*, pp. 92, 105.
52. *Ibid.*, pp. 128–129.
53. Donald L. Horowitz, *Ethnic Groups in Conflict*, p. 172.
54. Myron Weiner, *Sons of the Soil*, pp. 91–92.
55. *Ibid.*, p. 99.
56. *Ibid.*, p. 93.
57. Richard F. Nyrop, et al., *Area Handbook for India*, p. 508.
58. Myron Weiner, *Sons of the Soil*, pp. 103–104.
59. *Ibid.*, p. 91.
60. *Ibid.*, p. 104.
61. *Ibid.*, pp. 105–107.
62. Myron Weiner and Mary Fainsod Katzenstein, *India's Preferential Policies*, p. 96.
63. Myron Weiner, *Sons of the Soil*, p. 107.
64. *Ibid.*, p. 109.
65. *Ibid.*, p. 112.
66. *Ibid.*, pp. 108, 113.
67. *Ibid.*, pp. 124–125, 129.
68. *Ibid.*, pp. 118–119.
69. *Ibid.*, p. 127.
70. Myron Weiner and Mary Fainsod Katzenstein, *India's Preferential Policies*, p. 102.
71. *Ibid.*, p. 104.
72. *Ibid.*, p. 114.
73. *Ibid.*, p. 115.
74. *Ibid.*, p. 106.
75. *Ibid.*, pp. 120–121.
76. Michael T. Kaufman, "Death Toll in Assam Put at 1,127 as Counting of Votes Continues," *New York Times*, February 23, 1983, p. A4.
77. Mary Fainsod Katzenstein, *Ethnicity and Equality: The Shiv Sena Party and Preferential Policies in Bombay* (Ithaca: Cornell University Press, 1979), pp. 31–32.
78. Myron Weiner, *Sons of the Soil*, pp. 21–22, 24–25.
79. Mary Fainsod Katzenstein, *Ethnicity and Equality*, pp. 44–45.

80. Myron Weiner and Mary Fainsod Katzenstein, *India's Preferential Policies,* p. 52.
81. *Ibid.*, p. 48.
82. Mary Fainsod Katzenstein, *Ethnicity and Equality,* pp. 32–33.
83. *Ibid.*, p. 65.
84. *Ibid.*, pp. 47–48, 55.
85. *Ibid.*, pp. 47–48.
86. *Ibid.*, p. 33.
87. *Ibid.*, p. 49.
88. *Ibid.*, p. 73.
89. *Ibid.*, p. 72.
90. *Ibid.*, p. 99.
91. Richard F. Nyrop, et al., *Area Handbook for India,* p. 360.
92. *Ibid.*, p. 547.
93. Mary Fainsod Katzenstein, *Ethnicity and Equality,* p. 105.
94. *Ibid.*, p. 142.
95. *Ibid.*, p. 127.
96. Richard F. Nyrop, et al., *Area Handbook for India,* p. 360.
97. *Ibid.*, p. 549.
98. *Ibid.*, pp. 550–551.
99. Mary Anne Weaver, "Behind the Hindu-Muslim riots in India's Beleaguered Bombay," *Christian Science Monitor,* May 25, 1984, p. 7; "35 Reported Killed in New India Riots," *New York Times,* May 24, 1984, p. 3.
100. Mary Fainsod Katzenstein, *Ethnicity and Equality,* p. 35.
101. *Ibid.*, pp. 36, 191.
102. Myron Weiner and Mary Fainsod Katzenstein, *India's Preferential Policies,* p. 55.
103. *Ibid.*, pp. 47–48.
104. *Ibid.*, p. 48.
105. Mary Fainsod Katzenstein, *Ethnicity and Equality,* p. 142n.
106. Myron Weiner and Mary Fainsod Katzenstein, *India's Preferential Policies,* pp. 48–50.
107. *Ibid.*, p. 49.
108. *Ibid.*, pp. 52–53.
109. *Ibid.*, p. 122.
110. *Ibid.*, pp. 54–55.
111. *Ibid.*, p. 52.

112. Richard F. Nyrop, et al., *Area Handbook for India,* p. 94.
113. *The Times of India Directory Yearbook 1983,* p. 150.
114. *Ibid.,* pp. 108, 150.
115. *Ibid.,* p. 20.
116. *Ibid.,* pp. 236–237, 244.
117. Myron Weiner, *Sons of the Soil,* pp. 221–222, 238.
118. Myron Weiner and Mary Fainsod Katzenstein, *India's Preferential Policies,* p. 68.
119. Myron Weiner, *Sons of the Soil,* p. 229.
120. *Ibid.,* pp. 223–224.
121. Myron Weiner and Mary Fainsod Katzenstein, *India's Preferential Policies,* pp. 71–72.
122. Myron Weiner and Mary Fainsod Katzenstein, *India's Preferential Policies,* pp. 71–72.
123. *Ibid.,* pp. 74–75.
124. Myron Weiner, *Sons of the Soil,* p. 229.
125. *Ibid.,* p. 237n.
126. *Ibid.,* pp. 225–226.
127. *Ibid.,* p. 225.
128. *Ibid.,* p. 224.
129. *Ibid.,* p. 250.
130. *Ibid.,* pp. 253–255; Myron Weiner and Mary Fainsod Katzenstein, *India's Preferential Policies,* pp. 86–88.
131. Myron Weiner and Mary Fainsod Katzenstein, *India's Preferential Policies,* p. 218.
132. *Ibid.,* p. 84; Myron Weiner, *Sons of the Soil,* p. 219.
133. Myron Weiner, *Sons of the Soil,* p. 232.
134. *Ibid.,* p. 240.
135. *Ibid.,* pp. 253–255; Myron Weiner and Mary Fainsod Katzenstein, *India's Preferential Policies,* pp. 86–89.
136. Myron Weiner and Mary Fainsod Katzenstein, *India's Preferential Policies,* p. 121.
137. Colonial Office, *Nigeria: Report of the Commission appointed to enquire into the fears of Minorities and the Means of allaying them* (London: Her Majesty's Stationery Office, 1958), p. 54.
138. *Ibid.,* p. 53.
139. James S. Coleman, *Nigeria: Background to Nationalism* (Berkeley: University of California Press, 1965), p. 142.
140. Donald L. Horowitz, *Ethnic Groups in Conflict,* pp. 448, 451.

141. Northern Nigeria, *Statistical Yearbook 1965* (Kaduna: Ministry of Economic Planning, 1965), pp. 40–41.
142. A.H.M. Kirk-Greene, "A Training Course for Northern Nigeria Administrative Officers," *Journal of African Administration,* April 1959, p. 66.
143. Robert Melson and Howard Wolpe, *Nigeria: Modernization and the Politics of Communalism* (East Lansing: Michigan State University Press, 1971), p. 127.
144. Bernard Nkemdirim, "Social Change and the Genesis of Conflict in Nigeria," *Civilisations* (Belgium), Vol. 25, Nos. 1–2 (1975), p. 95.
145. Okwudiba Nnoli, *Ethnic Politics in Nigeria* (Enugu, Nigeria: Fourth Dimension Publishers, 1980), p. 64.
146. Bernard Nkemdirim, "Social Change and the Genesis of Conflict in Nigeria," *Civilisations,* Vol. 25, Nos. 1–2 (1975), p. 94.
147. A. Bamisaiye, "Ethnic Politics as an Instrument of Unequal Socio-Political Development in Nigeria's First Republic," *African Notes,* Vol. 6, no. 2, 1970–71, p. 101.
148. Okwudiba Nnoli, *Ethnic Politics in Nigeria,* pp. 117–118.
149. *Ibid.*, p. 189.
150. A. Bamisaiye, "Ethnic Politics as an Instrument of Unequal Socio-Political Development in Nigeria's First Republic," *African Notes,* Vol. 6, no. 2, 1970–71, pp. 102–103.
151. Robert O. Tilman and Taylor Cole, editors, *The Nigerian Political Scene* (Durham: Duke University Press, 1962), p. 108.
152. "Northern Nigeria's Holy War," *The Economist,* May 23, 1959, p. 745.
153. Professor Taylor Cole, "Bureaucracy in Transition: Independent Nigeria," *Public Administration,* Winter 1960, p. 334.
154. Larry Diamond, "Class, Ethnicity, and the Democratic State: Nigeria, 1950–1966," *Comparative Studies in Social History,* July 1983, p. 473.
155. L. H. Gann and Peter Duignan, editors, *Colonialism in Africa, 1870–1960,* Vol. II (Cambridge: Cambridge University Press, 1982), pp. 598–599; Okwudiba Nnoli, *Ethnic Politics in Nigeria,* p. 225; Dent Ocaya-Lakidi, "Black Atti-

tudes to the Brown and White Colonizers of East Africa," *Expulsion of a Minority: Essays on Ugandan Asians,* edited by Michael Twaddle (London: Institute of Commonwealth Studies, 1975), p. 81.

156. Larry Diamond, "Class, Ethnicity, and the Democratic State," *Comparative Studies in Social History,* July 1983, p. 462.
157. *Ibid.,* p. 474.
158. L. Adele Jinadu, "Federalism, The Consociational State, and Ethnic Conflict in Nigeria," *Publius,* Spring 1985, p. 81.
159. Larry Diamond, "Class, Ethnicity, and the Democratic State," *Comparative Studies in Social History,* July 1983, p. 459.
160. *Ibid.,* p. 469.
161. John A. A. Ayoade, "Ethnic Management in the 1979 Nigerian Constitution," *Canadian Review of Studies in Nationalism,* Spring 1987, pp. 124–125.
162. *Ibid.,* p. 141.
163. Martin Meredith, *The First Dance of Freedom: Black Africa in the Postwar Era* (New York: Harper & Row, 1984), pp. 207–208.
164. David Lamb, *The Africans* (New York: Random House, 1982), p. 308.
165. *Ibid.,* pp. 308–309.
166. Robert Melson and Howard Wolpe, editors, *Nigeria: Modernization and the Politics of Communalism,* pp. 129, 131.
167. L. Adele Jinadu, "Federalism, the Consociational State, and Ethnic Conflict in Nigeria," *Publius,* Spring 1985, pp. 88, 94.
168. James Brooke, "Nigeria's Ethnic Quotas for Schools and Jobs Face Challenge," *New York Times,* November 6, 1988, p. 19.
169. K. M. de Silva, "Historical Survey," *Sri Lanka: A Survey,* ed. K. M. de Silva (Honolulu: The University Press of Hawaii, 1977), p. 84.
170. "Sri Lanka had better prospects than most new states when independence came in 1948." Donald L. Horowitz, "A Splitting Headache," *The New Republic,* February 23, 1987, p. 33. "In general, relations among these main com-

munities in Ceylon are cordial, unmarred by the sort of friction that exists between Hindus and Moslems in India. Except for one sad episode in 1915, race riots have been unknown." Ronald N. Kearney, *Communalism and Language in the Politics of Ceylon,* (Durham: Duke University Press, 1967), p. 27; Walter Schwarz, *The Tamils of Sri Lanka* (London: Minority Rights Group, 1988), p. 6.

171. I.D.S. Weerawardana, "Minority Problems in Ceylon," *Pacific Affairs,* September 1952, p. 279.
172. H. A. Wyndham, *Native Education: Ceylon, Java, Formosa, the Philippines, French Indo-China, and British Malaya* (London: Oxford University Press, 1933), pp. 20–21.
173. Robert N. Kearney, "Language and the Rise of Tamil Separatism in Sri Lanka," *Asian Survey,* May 1978, p. 527.
174. Robert N. Kearney, *Communalism and Language in the Politics of Ceylon,* p. 66.
175. S. J. Tambiah, "Ethnic Representation in Ceylon's Higher Administrative Services, 1870–1946," *University of Ceylon Review,* Vol. 13 (1955), p. 130.
176. Robert N. Kearney, *Communalism and Language in the Politics of Ceylon,* p. 24; S. J. Tambiah, *Sri Lanka,* p. 66.
177. Robert N. Kearney, *Communalism and Language in the Politics of Ceylon,* p. 55.
178. C. R. de Silva, "Education," *Sri Lanka: A Survey,* ed. K. M. de Silva, p. 405.
179. S. J. Tambiah, "Ethnic Representation in Ceylon's Higher Administrative Services, 1870–1946," *University of Ceylon Review,* Vol. 13 (1955), p. 130.
180. *Ibid.*
181. *Ibid.,* pp. 131–132.
182. W. Ivor Jennings, "Race, Religion and Economic Opportunity in the University of Ceylon," *University of Ceylon Review,* November 1944, p. 2.
183. S.W.R. de A. Samarasinghe, "Ethnic Representation in Central Government Employment and Sinhala-Tamil Relations in Sri Lanka, 1948–1981," *From Independence to Freedom: Managing Ethnic Conflict in Five African and Asian States,* editors Robert B. Goldmann and A. Jeyaratnam Wilson (London: Frances Pinter, 1984), p. 177.

184. S. J. Tambiah, *Sri Lanka: Ethnic Fratricide and the Dismantling of Democracy* (Delhi: Oxford University Press, 1986), pp. 132–133.
185. *Ibid.*, pp. 71–72.
186. Robert N. Kearney, *Communalism and Language in the Politics of Ceylon*, p. 87.
187. *Ibid.*, Chapter VI.
188. Walter Schwarz, *The Tamils of Sri Lanka* (London: Minority Rights Group, 1983), pp. 9–10.
189. *Ibid.*
190. Robert N. Kearney, "Sinhalese Nationalism and Social Conflict in Ceylon," *Pacific Affairs*, Summer 1964, p. 130.
191. *Ibid.*, p. 135.
192. Chandra Richard de Silva, "Sinhala-Tamil Ethnic Rivalry: The Background," *From Independence to Statehood: Managing Ethnic Conflict in Five African and Asian States*, edited by Robert B. Goldmann and A. Jeyaratnam Wilson (London: Frances Pinter, 1984), p. 121.
193. Chandra Richard de Silva, "Sinhala-Tamil Relations and Education in Sri Lanka: The University Admissions Issue—The First Phase, 1971–7," *From Independence to Freedom*, p. 138. See also p. 127.
194. *Ibid.*, pp. 127–128.
195. *Ibid.*, pp. 129–131.
196. "Sri Lanka Confirms Report of Army Slayings," *New York Times*, August 7, 1983, Section 1, p. 5.
197. "The Unloveliness of Civil War," *The Economist*, August 18, 1984, p. 27.
198. S. J. Tambiah, *Sri Lanka*, p. 32.
199. Walter Schwarz, *The Tamils of Sri Lanka*, p. 6.
200. S. J. Tambiah, *Sri Lanka*, pp. 20–21, 26.
201. *Ibid.*, p. 20.
202. *Ibid.*, p. 22.
203. "India and the Tamils," *The Economist*, January 19, 1985, p. 35.
204. Mervyn De Silva, "Sri Lanka rebels defy Indian force, mediation," *The Christian Science Monitor*, July 21, 1988, p. 9.

205. D. John Grove, "Restructuring the Cultural Division of Labor in Malaysia and Sri Lanka," *Comparative Political Studies,* July 1986, pp. 190–193.
206. Leo Suryadinata, *Pribumi Indonesians, the Chinese Minority and China* (Singapore: Heinemann Asia, 1986), Chapter VI.
207. M. A. Tribe, "Economic Aspects of the Expulsion of Asians from Uganda," *Expulsion of a Minority: Essays on Ugandan Asians,* edited by Michael Twaddle, pp. 140–176.
208. R. S. Milne, *Politics in Ethnically Bipolar States* (Vancouver: University of British Columbia Press, 1981), pp. 143–145.
209. *Ibid.,* pp. 146–147.
210. David Lowenthal, *West Indian Societies* (New York: Oxford University Press, 1972), pp. 168–169.
211. H. L. van der Laan, *The Lebanese Traders in Sierra Leone* (The Hague: Mouton & Co., 1975), pp. 281–282, 291.
212. David Lowenthal, *West Indian Societies,* pp. 168–169.
213. Thomas Sowell, *The Economics and Politics of Race* (New York: William Morrow, 1983), p. 196.
214. "Facts on File: A Profile of 1987 Recipients of Doctorates," *The Chronicle of Higher Education,* March 15, 1989, p. A13.

Chapter 4: Minority Preferences in Majority Economies

1. Article 16, Section 4.
2. Partap C. Aggarwal and Mohd. Siddig Ashraf, *Equality Through Privilege: A Study of Special Privileges of Scheduled Castes in Haryana* (New Delhi: Shri Ram Centre for Industrial Relations and Human Resources, 1976), p. 4; Richard F. Nyrop, et al., *Area Handbook for India,* p. 51.
3. *Keesing's Contemporary Archives,* December 8, 1978, p. 29351.
4. *Report of the Commission for Scheduled Castes and Scheduled Tribes* (April 1979–March 1980), Second Report (New Delhi, 1981), p. 297.
5. *Report of the Commission for Scheduled Castes and Scheduled*

Tribes (July 1978–March 1979), First Report (New Delhi: Controller of Publications), p. 249.

6. See, for example, *Report of the Commission for Scheduled Castes and Scheduled Tribes* (April 1980–March 1981), p. 152; *Report of the Commission for Scheduled Castes and Scheduled Tribes* (April 1979–March 1980), pp. 349, 359; *Report of the Commission for Scheduled Castes and Scheduled Tribes* (July 1978–March 1979), p. 99.
7. *Report of the Commission for Scheduled Castes and Scheduled Tribes* (April 1981–March 1982), Fourth Report (New Delhi: 1983), p. 76.
8. *Ibid.*, p. 74.
9. Partap C. Aggarwal and Mohd. Siddig Ashraf, *Equality Through Privilege,* p. 49.
10. A. K. Vakil, *Reservation Policy and Scheduled Castes in India* (New Delhi: Ashish Publishing House, 1985), p. 117.
11. Barbara R. Joshi, " 'Ex-Untouchable': Problems, Progress, and Policies in Indian Social Change," *Pacific Affairs,* Summer 1980, pp. 196–197.
12. *Report of the Commission on Scheduled Castes and Scheduled Tribes* (April 1980–March 1981), Third Report (New Delhi, 1982), p. 148. See also Marc Galanter, *Competing Equalities: Law and the Backward Classes* (New Delhi: Oxford University Press, 1984), p. 15.
13. *Report of the Commission for Scheduled Castes and Scheduled Tribes* (April 1980–March 1981), Third Report (New Delhi: 1982), p. 151.
14. Partap C. Aggarwal and Mohd. Siddig Ashraf, *Equality Through Privilege,* p. 31.
15. K. M. de Silva, *Managing Ethnic Tensions in Multi-Ethnic Societies: Sri Lanka, 1880–1985* (Lanham, Maryland: University Press of America, 1986), p. 39.
16. Marc Galanter, *Competing Equalities,* p. 26n.
17. *Ibid.*, p. 33.
18. *Ibid.*, p. 36.
19. Suma Chitnis, "Education for Equality: Case of Scheduled Castes in Higher Education," *Economic and Political Weekly,* August 1972, Special Supplement, p. 1675. The numbers given are in "crores," meaning 10 million.

20. Barbara R. Joshi, " 'Ex-Untouchable': Problems, Progress, and Policies in India Social Change," *Pacific Affairs,* Summer 1980, p. 208.
21. Kusum K. Premi, "Educational Opportunities for the Scheduled Castes: Role of Protective Discrimination in Equalisation," *Economic and Political Weekly,* November 9, 1974, p. 1907.
22. Suma Chitnis, "Positive Discrimination in India with Reference to Education," *From Independence to Statehood: Managing Ethnic Conflict in Five African and Asian States,* ed. Robert B. Goldmann and A. Jeyaratnam Wilson (London: Frances Pinter, 1984), p. 37.
23. Padma Ramkrishna Velaskar, "Inequality in Higher Education: A Study of Scheduled Caste Students in Medical Colleges of Bombay," Ph.D. Dissertation, Tata Institute of Social Sciences, Bombay, 1986, p. 234.
24. *Ibid.,* p. 236.
25. Marc Galanter, *Competing Equalities,* pp. 64–65.
26. *Ibid.,* pp. 94–97.
27. P. R. Velaskar, "Inequality in Higher Education," p. 253.
28. *Ibid.,* p. 336.
29. *Ibid.,* pp. 334n, 337.
30. *Ibid.,* pp. 335.
31. Suma Chitnis, "Measuring up to Reserved Admissions," *Reservation: Policy, Programmes and Issues,* edited by Vimal P. Shah and Binod C. Agrawal (Jaipur, India: Rawat Publications, 1986), pp. 37–42.
32. P. R. Velaskar, "Inequality in Higher Education," p. 263.
33. *Ibid.,* p. 264.
34. *Report of the Commission for Scheduled Castes and Scheduled Tribes* (July 1978–March 1979), First Report, p. 188.
35. Ratna Murdia, "Issues in Positive Discrimination Policies for Disadvantaged Groups," *The Indian Journal of Social Work,* January 1983, p. 437; Suma Chitnis, "Education for Equality: Case of Scheduled Castes in Higher Education," *Economic and Political Weekly,* August 1972, p. 1676; Oliver

Mendelsohn, "A Harijan Elite? The Lives of Some Untouchable Politicians," *Economic and Political Weekly,* March 22, 1986, p. 504.

36. Suma Chitnis, "Positive Discrimination in India with Reference to Education," *From Independence to Statehood,* ed. Robert B. Goldmann and A. Jeyaratnam Wilson, p. 36.
37. Marc Galanter, *Competing Equalities,* p. 63.
38. P. R. Velaskar, "Inequality in Higher Education," p. 312.
39. *Ibid.*, Chapter VI, passim.
40. *Ibid.*, p. 355.
41. A. K. Vakil, *Reservation Policy and Scheduled Castes in India,* p. 138.
42. Jacob Aikara, *Scheduled Castes and Higher Education,* p. 15.
43. *Ibid.*, pp. 91, 138.
44. Barbara R. Joshi, "Whose Law, Whose Order: 'Untouchables' Social Violence and the State in India," *Asian Survey,* July 1982, pp. 680, 682.
45. A. K. Vakil, *Reservation Policy and Scheduled Castes in India,* p. 67; Ghagat Ram Goyal, *Educating Harijans* (Gurgaon, Haryana: The Academic Press, 1981), p. 21.
46. George J. Bryak, "Collective Violence in India," *Asian Affairs,* Summer 1986, p. 41.
47. Ti Hamaguchi, "Some Explanations of the Violence during the Anti-Reservation Agitation in Gujarat," *Indian Journal of Politics,* July–December 1986, p. 7.
48. R. S. Morkhandikar, "Marathwada Riots 1978: Dilemmas of a Dalit Movement," *Punjab Journal of Politics,* January–June 1985, p. 43.
49. *Report of the Commission for Scheduled Castes and Scheduled Tribes,* July 1978–March 1979, First Report, p. 85.
50. Marc Galanter, *Competing Equalities,* pp. 44, 46.
51. Upendra Baxi, "Legislative Reservations for Social Justice: Some Thoughts on India's Unique Experiment," *From Independence to Statehood,* ed. Robert B. Goldmann and A. Jeyaratnam Wilson, pp. 215–216. See also M. Satyanarayana and Rao and G. Srinivas Reddy, "Political Representation:

National, State and Local," *Reservation Policy in India,* edited by B.A.V. Sharma and K. Madhusudhan Reddy (New Delhi: Light & Life Publishers, 1982), pp. 365–367.

52. B. Sivaramayya, "Affirmative Action: The Scheduled Castes and the Scheduled Tribes," International Conference on Affirmative Action, Bellagio Conference Center; Bellagio, Italy, August 16–20, 1982, p. 2.
53. Marc Galanter, *Competing Equalities,* p. 338.
54. *Ibid.*, pp. 86–87.
55. *Ibid.*, p. 88.
56. *Ibid.*, p. 89.
57. *Ibid.*, pp. 90–91, 96.
58. *Ibid.*, pp. 108–109.
59. Uma Ramaswamy, "Protection and Inequality among Backward Groups," *Economic and Political Weekly,* March 1, 1986, pp. 401–402.
60. Marc Galanter, *Competing Equalities,* pp. 100, 101.
61. *Ibid.*, p. 101.
62. *Ibid.*, p. 113n.
63. *Report of the Commission on Scheduled Castes and Scheduled Tribes* (July 1978–March 1979), First Report, p. 230.
64. A. K. Vakil, *Reservation Policy and Scheduled Castes in India,* p. 70.
65. Nathan Glazer, *Affirmative Discrimination* (New York: Basic Books, Inc., 1975), p. 45.
66. See, for example, U.S. Equal Employment Opportunity Commission, *Legislative History of Titles VII and XI of Civil Rights Act of 1964* (Washington, D.C.: U.S. Government Printing Office, no date), pp. 3005, 3006, 3013, 3015, 3134, 3160, 3187–3190.
67. Section 703(j).
68. *Regents of the University of California* v. *Allan Bakke,* 438 U.S. 265.
69. *United Steelworkers of America* v. *Brian Weber,* 443 U.S. 193.
70. *Fullilove* v. *Klutznick,* 448 U.S. 448 (1980).

71. *City of Richmond* v. *J. A. Croson Co.*, 89 California Daily Opinion Service, 582.
72. John H. Bunzel, "Affirmative-Action Admission: How It 'Works' at U.C. Berkeley," *The Public Interest*, Fall 1988, p. 122.
73. Thomas Sowell, *Choosing A College: A Guide for Parents and Students* (New York: Harper & Row, 1989), p. 63.
74. *America's Best Colleges: 1990.* (Washington, D.C.: U.S. News & World Report, 1989), pp. 52–57, 59.
75. Robert Klitgaard, *Choosing Elites* (New York: Basic Books, Inc., 1985), p. 175.
76. For example, *Ibid.*, pp. 104–131; Stanley Sue and Jennifer Abe, *Predictors of Academic Achievement Among Asian Students and White Students* (New York: College Entrance Examination Board, 1988), p. 1; T. Anne Cleary, "Test Bias: Predictions of Grades of Negro and White Students in Integrated Colleges," *Journal of Educational Measurement*, Summer 1966, pp. 115–124; J. C. Stanley and A. L. Porter, "Correlation of Scholastic Aptitude Test Scores with College Grades for Negros vs. Whites," *Journal of Educational Measurement*, 1969, pp. 199–218.
77. Robert Klitgaard, *Choosing Elites*, pp. 104–115; Stanley Sue and Jennifer Abe, *Predictors of Academic Achievement Among Asian American and White Students*, p. 1; Arthur R. Jensen, "Selection of Minority Students in Higher Education," *University of Toledo Law Review*, Spring–Summer 1970, pp. 440, 443; Donald A. Rock, "Motivation, Moderators, and Test Bias," *ibid.*, pp. 536, 537; Ronald L. Flaugher, *Testing Practices, Minority Groups and Higher Education: A Review and Discussion of the Research* (Princeton: Educational Testing Service, 1970), p. 11.
78. Stanley Sue and Jennifer Abe, *Predictors of Academic Achievement Among Asian American and White Students*, p. 8.
79. Quoted in John H. Bunzel, "Affirmative-Action Admission: How It 'Works' at U.C. Berkeley," *The Public Interest*, p. 118.

80. *Ibid.*, p. 123.
81. *Ibid.*, p. 124.
82. Thomas Sowell, "The New Racism on Campus," *Fortune,* February 13, 1989, pp. 115–116.
83. Shelby Steele, "The Recoloring of Campus Life," *Harper's* magazine, February 1989, p. 52.
84. Robert Klitgaard, *Choosing Elites,* p. 160.
85. *Ibid.*, p. 162.
86. Computed from National Research Council, *Summary Report 1982: Doctorate Recipients from United States Universities* (Washington, D.C.: National Academy Press, 1983), p. 30
87. Computed from *Ibid.*, pp. 30, 33.
88. Computed from *Ibid.*, pp. 30, 32.
89. Robert Higgs, *Competition and Coercion* (Cambridge: Cambridge University Press, 1977), p. 117.
90. Thomas Sowell, *Ethnic America* (New York: Basic Books, Inc., 1981), pp. 210, 212–213.
91. U.S. Commission on Civil Rights, *The Economic Progress of Black Men in America* (Washington, D.C.: U.S. Commission on Civil Rights, 1986), p. 11.
92. Thomas Sowell, *Civil Rights: Rhetoric or Reality?* (New York: William Morrow and Company, Inc., 1984), p. 49.
93. James P. Smith and Finis Welch, *Race Difference in Earnings: A Survey and New Evidence* (Santa Monica: The Rand Corporation, 1978), pp. 19–21.
94. *Ibid.*, pp. 24, 49.
95. Finis Welch, "Affirmative Action and Its Enforcement," *American Economic Review,* May 1981, p. 132.
96. "Yet, despite the vast sums expended, the high cost of Government intervention in the provision of social services has not had the intended effects of improving Maori performance at school or in the labour force." Augie J. Fleras, "From Social Welfare to Community Development: Maori Policy and the Development of Maori Affairs in New Zealand," *Community Development Journal,* January 1984, p. 38.
97. Thomas Sowell, "Ethnicity in A Changing America," *Daedalus,* Winter 1978, p. 214.
98. Thomas Sowell, *Civil Rights: Rhetoric or Reality?* (New York: William Morrow, 1984), p. 51.

99. *Ibid.*
100. *Ibid.*, pp. 80–81.
101. Charles Murray, *Losing Ground: American Social Policy, 1950–1980* (New York: Basic Books, Inc., 1984), p. 87.
102. Sammy Smooha and Yochanan Peres, "The Dynamics of Ethnic Inequalities: The Case of Israel," *Studies of Israeli Society,* ed. Ernest Krausz (New Brunswick: Transaction Books, 1981), p. 173.

Chapter 5: The Illusion of Control and Knowledge

1. Quoted in Alan Little and Diana Robbins, *'Loading the Law'* (London: Commission for Racial Equality, 1982), p. 6.
2. Sham Satish Chandra Misra, *Preferential Treatment in Public Employment and Equality of Opportunity* (Lucknow: Eastern Book Company, 1979), p. 83.
3. Donald L. Horowitz, *Ethnic Groups in Conflict* (Berkeley: University of California Press, 1985), p. 657.
4. Charles H. Kennedy, "Policies of Redistributional Preference in Pakistan," *Ethnic Preference and Public Policy in Developing States,* edited by Neil Nevitte and Charles H. Kennedy (Boulder: Lynn Rienner Publishers, Inc., 1986), p. 69; see also pp. 64–65, 68.
5. *Ibid.*, p. 64.
6. Donald L. Horowitz, *Ethnic Groups in Conflict,* p. 242.
7. Charles H. Kennedy, "Policies of Redistributional Preference in Pakistan," *Ethnic Preference and Public Policy in Developing States,* edited by Neil Nevitte and Charles H. Kennedy, p. 69.
8. *Ibid.*, p. 93.
9. Women alone are 52 percent of the U.S. population. To these must be added black, Hispanic, and American Indian males, as well as the male elderly.
10. Nathan Glazer, *Ethnic Dilemmas: 1964–1982* (Cambridge, Massachusetts: Harvard University Press, 1983), pp. 9–10.
11. John A. A. Ayoade, "Ethnic Management in the 1979 Nigerian Constitution," *Canadian Review of Studies in Nationalism,* Spring 1987, p. 127.

12. W. H. Hutt, *The Economics of the Colour Bar* (London: Institute of Economic Affairs, 1964), p. 63.
13. Margaret A. Gibson, "Ethnicity and Schooling: West Indian Immigrants in the United States Virgin Island," *Ethnic Groups,* Vol. 5, No. 3 (1983), pp. 190, 191, 192.
14. Donald L. Horowitz, *Ethnic Groups in Conflict,* p. 670.
15. Daniel C. Thompson, *Private Black Colleges at the Crossroads,* (Westport, Connecticut: Greenwood Press, 1973), p. 88.
16. A. K. Vakil, *Reservation Policy and Scheduled Castes in India* (New Delhi: Ashish Publishing House, 1985), p. 147.
17. W. H. Hutt, *The Economics of the Colour Bar,* p. 79.
18. Carol S. Holzbery, *Minorities and Power in a Black Society: The Jewish Community of Jamaica* (Lanham, Maryland: the North-South Publishing Co., Inc., 1987), p. 420.
19. Thomas Sowell, "The New Racism on Campus," *Fortune,* February 13, 1989, pp. 115–120.
20. See, for example, K. M. de Silva, *Managing Ethnic Tensions in Multi-Ethnic Societies: Sri Lanka, 1880–1985* (Lanham, Maryland: University Press of America, 1986), Chapter XVII.
21. James Blanton, "A Limit to Affirmative Action?" *Commentary,* June 1989, p. 31.
22. See, for example, William Moore, Jr., and Lonnie H. Wagstaff, *Black Educators in White Colleges* (San Francisco: Jossey-Bass Publishing Co., 1974), pp. 130–131, 198.
23. J. W. Foster, "Race and Truth at Harvard," *New Republic,* July 16, 1976, pp. 16–20.
24. A. K. Vakil, *Reservation Policy and Scheduled Castes in India,* p. 137.
25. David Riesman, *On Higher Education: The Academic Enterprise in an Age of Rising Student Consumerism* (San Francisco: Jossey-Bass Publishers, 1980), pp. 80–81.
26. Thomas Sowell, *Black Education: Myths and Tragedies* (New York: David McKay Co., 1972), pp. 131–132, 140.
27. Nancy Lubin, *Labour and Nationality in Soviet Central Asia: An Uneasy Compromise* (Princeton: Princeton University Press, 1984), p. 162.
28. Gordon P. Means, "Ethnic Preference Policies in Malaysia," *Ethnic Preference and Public Policy in Developing*

States, edited by Neil Nevitte and Charles H. Kennedy (Boulder: Lynne Reinner Publishers, Inc., 1986), p. 108.

29. *United Steelworkers of America* v. *Weber,* 443 U.S. 193 (1979), at 365–366, 374, n. 58.

30. Thomas Sowell, "Ethnicity in A Changing America," *Daedalus,* Winter 1978, pp. 225–227.

31. See, for example, Yuan-li Wu and Chun-hsi Wu, *Economic Development in Southeast Asia* (Stanford: Hoover Institution Press, 1980), pp. 84, 87; Jacques Amyot, *The Manila Chinese: Familism in the Philippine Environment* (Quezon City, Philippines: Institute of Philippine Culture, 1973), p. 4; Edith Laikin Elkin, *Jews of the Latin American Republics* (Chapel Hill: University of North Carolina Press, 1980), pp. 192–194; Daniel J. Elazar, *Jewish Communities in Frontier Societies: Argentina, Australia and South Africa* (New York: Holmes & Meier, 1983), pp. 7, 262; William O. McCagg, Jr., *A History of the Hapsburg Jews* (Bloomington: Indiana University Press, 1989), p. 11; Arthur A. Gorem, "Jews," *Harvard Encyclopedia of American Ethnic Groups* (Cambridge, Massachusetts: Harvard University Press, 1981), p. 592.

32. Samuel L. Baily, "The Adjustment of Italian Immigrants in Buenos Aires and New York, 1870–1914," *American Historical Review,* April 1983, p. 291.

33. Mary Fainsod Katzenstein, *Ethnicity and Equality,* pp. 31–32.

34. Or misunderstood *yet again* in my case. See Thomas Sowell, *Civil Rights: Rhetoric or Reality?* (New York: William Morrow and Company, Inc., 1984), p. 128.

35. It is described as a "work of breathtaking scope and prodigious scholarship" and "certain to become a classic" in the *Journal of Modern African Studies,* March 1987, pp. 117, 128. It is called "a massive and important study" that is "indispensable" in the *Columbia Law Review,* March 1986, p. 427. The book's reasoning is characterized as "penetrating" and "supported by an impressive battery of documentation" in *Man,* September 1986, p. 570. The "wealth of detailed evidence with which the arguments are buttressed" is also mentioned in a review which calls Horowitz's book "a landmark," *Government and Opposition,* Spring 1987, pp. 254, 256.

36. Donald L. Horowitz, *Ethnic Groups in Conflict,* p. 677.

37. Cynthia H. Enloe, *Police, Military and Ethnicity: Foundations of State Power* (New Brunswick: Transaction Books, 1980), p. 143.
38. *Ibid.*, p. 163.
39. *Ibid.*, p. 37.
40. *Ibid.*, p. 144.
41. *Ibid.*, p. 56.
42. *Ibid.*, pp. 75, 84.
43. Moses Rischin, *The Promised City: New York's Jews 1870–1914* (Cambridge, Massachusetts, 1962), pp. 61–68; Judith Laikin Elkin, *Jews of the Latin American Republics* (Chapel Hill: University of North Carolina Press, 1980), pp. 110, 115.
44. Simon Kuznets, "Immigration of Russian Jews to the United States: Background and Structure," *Perspectives in American History,* Vol. IX (1975), p. 76.
45. Daniel J. Elazar, *Jewish Communities in Frontier Societies* (New York: Holmes & Meier, 1983), p. 243.
46. Thomas Huebner, *The Germans in America* (Radnor, Pennsylvania: Chilton Co., 1962), p. 128; W. D. Borrie, *Italians and Germans in Australia* (Melbourne: The Australian National University, 1934), p. 94; Alfred Dolge, *Pianos and Their Makers* (Covina, California: Covina Publishing Co., 1911), pp. 172, 264; Edwin M. Good, *Giraffes, Black Dragons, and Other Pianos: A Technological History from Cristofi to the Modern Concert Grand* (Stanford: Stanford University Press, 1982), p. 137n.
47. Myron Weiner, "The Pursuit of Ethnic Inequalities Through Preferential Policies: A Comparative Public Policy Perspective," *From Independence to Statehood,* edited by Robert B. Goldmann and A. Jeyaratnam Wilson (London: Frances Pinter, 1984), p. 64.
48. Peter Uhlenberg, "Demographic Correlates of Group Achievement: Contrasting Patterns of Mexican-Americans and Japanese-Americans," *Race, Creed, Color, or National Origin,* edited by Robert K. Yin (Itasca, Illinois: F. E. Peacock Publishers, Inc., 1973) p. 91.
49. Andrew Greeley, *That Most Distressful Nation: The Taming of the American Irish* (Chicago: Quadrangle Books, 1972), p. 132.

50. Thomas Sowell, *Civil Rights,* p. 18.
51. *Ibid.*, p. 19.
52. Philip E. Vernon, *Intelligence and Cultural Environment* (London: Methuen & Co. Ltd., 1970); *idem, The Abilities and Achievements of Orientals in North America* (New York: Academic Press, 1982).
53. U.S. Commission on Civil Rights, *Unemployment and Underemployment Among Blacks, Hispanics, and Women* (Washington, D.C.: U.S. Commission on Civil Rights, 1982), p. 58.
54. Mohamed Suffian bin Hashim, "Problems and Issues of Higher Education Development in Malaysia," *Development of Higher Education in Southeast Asia: Problems and Issues* (Singapore: Regional Institute of Higher Education and Development, 1973), pp. 56–78; Chandra Richard de Silva, "Sinhala-Tamil Relations and Education in Sri Lanka: The University Admissions Issue—The First Phase, 1971–7," *From Independence to Statehood: Managing Ethnic Conflict in Five African and Asian States,* edited by R. B. Goldman and A. J. Wilson (London: Frances Pinter, 1984), pp. 125–146; Sammy Smooha and Yochanan Peres, "The Dynamics of Ethnic Equality: the Case of Israel," *Studies of Israeli Society,* edited by Ernest Krausz, (New Brunswick: Transaction Books, 1980), p. 173; Suma Chitnis, "Positive Discrimination in India With Reference to Education," *From Independence to Statehood,* pp. 31–43; Thomas Sowell, "Ethnicity in A Changing America," *Daedalus,* Winter 1978, pp. 231–232.
55. Thomas Sowell, *Education: Assumptions versus History* (Stanford: Hoover Institution Press, 1986), pp. 83, 85, 86, 87.
56. *Ibid.*
57. *Ibid.*
58. Padma Ramkrishna Velaskar, "Inequality in Higher Education: A Study in Scheduled Caste Students in Medical Colleges of Bombay," Ph.D. thesis, Tata Institute of Social Sciences, Bombay, 1986, p. 357.
59. *Ibid.*, p. 366.
60. *Ibid.*, pp. 391, 396.
61. *Ibid.*, p. 406.
62. *Ibid.*, p. 414.

63. *Ibid.*, p. 418.
64. Thomas Sowell, *Civil Rights: Rhetoric or Reality* (New York: William Morrow & Co., 1984), pp. 49–56.
65. *Ibid.*, p. 50.
66. Myron Weiner and Mary Fainsod Katzenstein, *India's Preferential Policies: Migrants, The Middle Classes, and Ethnic Equality* (Chicago: University of Chicago Press, 1981), p. 54.
67. *Ibid.*, pp. 54, 55.
68. Celia Heller, *On the Edge of Destruction: Jews of Poland Between the Two World Wars* (New York: Columbia University Press, 1987), pp. 16, 17, 107, 123–128; Ezra Mendelsohn, *The Jews of East Central Europe Between the World Wars* (Bloomington: Indiana University Press, 1983), pp. 99, 105, 167, 232, 236–237.
69. Larry Diamond, "Class, Ethnicity, and the Democratic State: Nigeria, 1950–1966," *Comparative Studies in Social History,* July 1983, pp. 462, 473.
70. Donald L. Horowitz, *Ethnic Groups in Conflict* (Berkeley: University of California Press, 1985), pp. 221–226; Myron Weiner and Mary Fainsod Katzenstein, *India's Preferential Policies,* pp. 4–5, 132; Myron Weiner, "The Pursuit of Ethnic Equality Through Preferential Policies: A Comparative Public Policy Perspective," *From Independence to Statehood,* ed. R. B. Goldmann and A. J. Wilson, p. 78; K. M. de Silva, "University Admissions and Ethnic Tensions in Sri Lanka," *Ibid.*, pp. 125–126; Donald V. Smiley, "French-English Relations in Canada and Consociational Democracy," *Ethnic Conflict in the Western World,* edited by Milton J. Esman (Ithaca: Cornell University Press, 1977), pp. 186–188.
71. Myron Weiner and Mary Fainsod Katzenstein, *India's Preferential Policies* (Chicago: University of Chicago Press, 1981), pp. 53, 123, 124, 125; Raphael Mahler, "Jews in Public Service and the Liberal Professions in Poland, 1918–39," *Jewish Social Studies,* October 1944, pp. 291–350; Tai Yoke Lin, "Inter-Ethnic Restructuring in Malaysia, 1970–1980: The Employment Perspective," *From Independence to Statehood,* ed. R. B. Goldmann and A. J. Wilson, pp. 47–48, 51, 54; Pang Eng Fong, "Race, Income Distribution, and Development in Malaysia and Singapore," *The Chinese in South-*

east Asia, ed. Peter Gosling and Linda Y. C. Lim, (Singapore: Maruzen Asia, 1983), p. 317; Yeshuda Don, "The Economic Dimension of Anti-Semitism: Anti-Jewish Legislation in Hungary, 1938–1944," *East European Quarterly,* January 1987, p. 456; S.W.R. de A. Samarasinghe, "Ethnic Representation in Central Government Employment and Sinhala-Tamil Relations in Sri Lanka, 1948–81," *From Independence to Statehood,* ed. Goldmann and Wilson, pp. 173–184.; James P. Smith and Finis Welch, "Affirmative Action and Labor Markets," *Journal of Labor Economics,* April 1984, p. 297.

72. James P. Smith and Finis Welch, "Affirmative Action and Labor Markets," *Journal of Labor Economics,* April 1984, p. 282.
73. Thomas Sowell, *Race and Economics* (New York: David McKay Co., 1975), pp. 182–183.
74. Thomas Sowell, *Ethnic America* (New York: Basic Books, 1981), pp. 212–213.

Chapter 6: The Illusion of Morality and Compensation

1. Peter S. Li, "Income Achievement and Adaptive Capacity: An Empirical Comparison of Chinese and Japanese in Canada," *Visible Minorities and Multiculturalism: Asians in Canada,* edited by K. Victor Ujimoto and Gordon Hirabayashi (Toronto: Butterworths and Company Limited, 1980), p. 365; Thomas Sowell, *Ethnic America* (New York: Basic Books, 1981), pp. 162–163, 165–166, 171–172.
2. Herbert G. Gutman, *The Black Family in Slavery and Freedom, 1750–1925* (New York: Vintage Books, 1977).
3. Thomas Sowell, *The Economics and Politics of Race: An International Perspective* (New York: William Morrow & Co., Inc., 1983), p. 193.
4. W. H. Hutt, *The Economics of the Colour Bar* (London: André Deutsch, 1964), p. 42.
5. *Ibid.,* p. 39.
6. Mary Fainsod Katzenstein, *Ethnicity and Equality: The Shiv*

Sena Party and Preferential Policies in Bombay (Ithaca: Cornell University Press, 1979), p. 138.

7. Dent Ocaya-Lakidi, "Black Attitudes to the Brown and White Colonizers of East Africa," *Expulsion of a Minority: Essays on Ugandan Asians,* edited by Michael Twaddle (London: The Athlone Press, 1975), pp. 81–97.
8. Okwudiba Nnoli, *Ethnic Politics in Nigeria* (Enugu, Nigeria: Fourth Dimension Publishing Co. Ltd., 1978), pp. 224–225.
9. Donald L. Horowitz, *Ethnic Groups in Conflict* (Berkeley: University of California Press, 1985), p. 113.
10. *Ibid.,* pp. 115–116.
11. *Ibid.,* pp. 117–118.
12. *Ibid.,* p. 118.
13. *Ibid.,* p. 118.
14. *Ibid.,* p. 121.
15. *Ibid.,* pp. 115–116; Jack Chen, *The Chinese of America* (San Francisco: Harper & Row, 1980), p. 109.
16. Robert N. Kearney, *Communalism and Language in the Politics of Ceylon* (Durham: University of North Carolina Press, 1967), p. 71.
17. Donald L. Horowitz, *Ethnic Groups in Conflict,* p. 225.
18. Nathaniel Katzburg, *Hungary and the Jews: Policy and Legislation 1920–1943* (Jerusalem: Bar-Ilan University Press, 1981), p. 20.
19. Robert C. Nichols, "Heredity, Environment, and School Achievement," *Measurement and Evaluation in Guidance,* Summer 1968, p. 126.
20. Marc Galanter, *Competing Equalities: Law and the Backward Classes in India* (Delhi: Oxford University Press, 1984), p. 469.
21. Ozay Mehmet, "An Empirical Evaluation of Government Scholarship Policy in Malaysia," *Higher Education* (The Netherlands), April 1985, p. 202.
22. Chandra Richard de Silva, "Sinhala-Tamil Relations in Sri Lanka: The University Admissions Issue—The First Phase, 1971–1977," *From Independence to Statehood,* edited by Robert B. Goldmann and A. Jeyaratnam Wilson (London: Frances Pinter, 1984), p. 133.

23. Lim Mah Hui, "The Ownership and Control of Large Corporations in Malaysia: The Role of Chinese Businessmen," *The Chinese in Southeast Asia,* Vol. I, Peter Gosling and Linda Y. C. Lim, eds. (Singapore: Maruzen Asia, 1983), pp. 281, 284, 308.
24. Mavis Puthucheary, "Public Policies Relating to Business and Land, and Their Impact on Ethnic Relations in Peninsular Malaysia", in Robert B. Goldmann and A. Jeyaratnam Wilson, eds., *From Independence to Statehood,* p. 158.
25. Marc Galanter, *Competing Equalities,* p. 89.
26. B. Sivaramaya, "Affirmative Action: The Scheduled Castes and the Scheduled Tribes," International Conference on Affirmative Action, Bellagio Conference Center, Bellagio, Italy, August 16–20, 1982, p. 25.
27. Finis Welch, "Affirmative Action and Its Enforcement," *American Economic Review,* May 1981, p. 132.
28. Rep. David Dreir, " 'Disadvantaged' Contractors' Unfair Advantage," *Wall Street Journal,* February 21, 1989, p. A18.
29. Myron Weiner and Mary Fainsod Katzenstein, *India's Preferential Policies* (Chicago: University of Chicago Press, 1981), p. 52.
30. Ezra Mendelsohn, *The Jews of East Central Europe Between the World Wars* (Bloomington: Indiana University Press, 1983), p. 122.
31. Donald L. Horowitz, *Ethnic Groups in Conflict,* p. 666.
32. Celia S. Heller, *On the Edge of Destruction: Jews of Poland Between the Two World Wars* (New York: Columbia University Press, 1987), p. 102.
33. Maria S. Muller, "The National Policy of Kenyanisation: Its Impact on a Town in Kenya," *Canadian Journal of African Studies,* Vol. 15, No. 2 (1981), p. 298.
34. "Indians: In the Red," *The Economist,* February 25, 1989, pp. 25–26.
35. Chris Miles, "Aboriginal Affairs: Information Guide for Coalition Members," Canberra, November 1987, mimeographed, pp. 1–2.
36. James Brooke, "Nigeria's Ethnic Quotas for Schools and Jobs Face Challenge," *New York Times,* November 6, 1988, p. 19.

37. K. M. de Silva, "University Admissions and Ethnic Tension in Sri Lanka, 1977–82," *From Independence to Statehood,* eds. R. B. Goldman and A. Jeyaratnam Wilson, p. 97.
38. See Chapter 4 of this book.
39. Suma Chitnis, "Positive Discrimination in India with Reference to Education," *From Independence to Statehood,* ed. Robert B. Goldman and A. Jeyaratnam Wilson, p. 36; Nancy Lubin, *Labour and Nationalism in Soviet Central Asia: An Uneasy Compromise* (Princeton: Princeton University Press, 1984), pp. 120–121; Thomas Sowell, *The Economics and Politics of Race,* pp. 139–140. See also p. 47 of this book.
40. Lelah Dushkin, "Backward Class Benefits and Social Class in India, 1920–1970," *Economic and Political Weekly,* April 7, 1979, p. 666.
41. In some years the number of people killed in these riots has exceeded the number of untouchables actually using the medical school quotas.
42. *Regents of the University of California* v. *Allan Bakke,* 438 U.S. 265.
43. *City of Richmond* v. *Croson Co.,* 109 S.Ct. 706 (1989).
44. Marc Galanter, *Competing Equalities,* pp. 501–502.
45. John H. Bunzel, "Prepared, Not Preferred," *Stanford Magazine,* Fall/Winter 1980, pp. 58–61.

Chapter 7: Replacing Illusions

1. Donald Horowitz, *Ethnic Groups in Conflict* (Berkeley: University of California Press, 1985), p. 677.
2. Whether or not that is true is an empirical question. More broadly, who in fact benefits in any country from any preference is an empirical question.
3. "Cajuns Ask Minority Status," *New York Times,* May 23, 1988, p. A14.
4. D. L. Sheth, "Reservations Policy Revisited," *Economic and Political Weekly,* November 14, 1987, p. 1959.
5. William Kerley, "From Land Rights to Separatism," *IPA Review,* November–January 1987/1988, p. 16.

6. "Racism 'Not Changed' Says Professor," *The Press* (Christchurch, New Zealand), September 23, 1988, p. 6.
7. William Kerley, "From Land Rights to Separatism," *IPA Review,* November–January 1987/1988, p. 16.
8. Pat Dodson, "Giant Jigsaw Puzzle," *New Internationalist,* August 1988, p. 10.
9. Ken Baker, "A Treaty Would Divide Australia," *IPA Review,* November–January 1987/1988, p. 20.
10. John Marks, " 'Anti-Racism'—Revolution Not Education," *Anti-Racism—An Assault on Education and Value,* editor Frank Palmer (London: The Sherwood Press, 1986), pp. 34–35.
11. See for example, the various essays in *Anti-racism—An Assault on Education and Value* (London: The Sherwood Press, 1986) for an account of this phenomenon in Britain. A careful critique of a similar phenomenon in the very different setting of American legal scholarship is Randall L. Kennedy, "Racial Critiques of Legal Academia," *Harvard Law Review,* Vol. 102, No. 8 (June 1989), pp. 1745–1819.
12. Donald Horowitz, *Ethnic Groups in Conflict,* p. 171; see also pp. 167–181.
13. *Mid-term Review of the Fourth Malaysia Plan 1981–1985* (Kuala Lumpur, Government Press, 1984), p. 17.
14. Nathaniel Katzburg, *Hungary and the Jews: Policy and Legislation, 1920–1943* (Jerusalem: Bar-Ilan University Press, 1981), p. 234.
15. Thomas Sowell, *Ethnic America: A History* (New York: Basic Books, 1981), p. 59.
16. See, for example, James M. McPherson, *The Abolitionist Legacy* (Princeton: Princeton University Press, 1975); Thomas Sowell, "Patterns of Black Excellence," *The Public Interest,* Spring 1976, pp. 26–58.
17. Kathryn G. Caird, "A Note on the Progress of Preference Students in First Year Accounting Courses," internal memorandum, University of Auckland (undated but probably 1989).

INDEX

INDEX

Index